Advance praise ...

Can Francis Change the Church?

"Tom Sweetser's research has brought the voice of the people into a much needed conversation. More than anything, the People of God connect to the longing of Pope Francis to take seriously what Jesus took seriously: inclusion, non-violence, unconditional, loving kindness and acceptance. This invaluable book reminds us that we all want the same things."

—Gregory Boyle, SJ,
Founding Director, Homeboy Industries

"The 'before and after Francis' method of interviewing has opened the door to a much more creative treatment of the topic: it reveals not only what people think but also how a leader might influence that thinking and why. Though the responses of this very readable study come from only a sampling of interviewees, they provide the kind of insight that those working in and for local parishes cannot afford to ignore."

—Dianne Bergant, CSA

"Thanks to experience both deep and long, Tom Sweetser, SJ, knows what works (and what doesn't) in parish life. He brings this wisdom to his new book about how Pope Francis is changing the Catholic Church by uncovering the attitudes and feelings of two groups: those who struggle but have remained Catholics, and those who have left the Church. This is a surprising, insightful and moving book for reflection, prayer and discussion."

—James Martin, SJ,
author of *Jesus: A Pilgrimage*

"What a wonderful combination of heartfelt reflection, significant data and assessment of timely and relevant issues pertaining to the Catholic Church. The author presents a wealth of practical, pastoral suggestions for the renewal and growth of the parish and larger Church. May we all follow the example of Pope Francis by making a difference through the faith, work, and example in our lives!"

—Kate DeVries,
Pastoral Associate & Young Adult Minister,
Archdiocese of Chicago

"Fr. Tom Sweetser has given us a thoughtful and accessible book on what ordinary Catholics think about their Church. With decades of experience in parish research and renewal he has listened carefully to dozens of people who have distanced themselves from church life and also who remain. The result is a revelatory presentation and analysis of the thoughts and questions of a cross-section of American Catholics both 'before and after' the election of Pope Francis."

—Brett C. Hoover, Ph.D.,
Associate Professor of Pastoral and Practical Theology,
Loyola Marymount University,
author of *The Shared Parish: Latinos, Anglos,
and the Future of US Catholicism*

"For over forty years, Tom Sweetser, SJ, has been in the trenches of Catholic parish life. Here, from a host of witnesses and with hard-won wisdom, he honestly portrays the choking weeds and hopeful seeds for our Catholic faith, with the jury still out on whether Francis can 'save the Church.' This is a confrontational and rich resource for the nones, the dones, and those of us still hopeful."

—Thomas Groome,
Professor of Theology & Religious Education,
Director of Ph.D. in Theology and
Education, Boston College

CAN FRANCIS CHANGE THE CHURCH?

CAN FRANCIS CHANGE THE CHURCH?

How American Catholics Are Responding to His Leadership

Thomas P. Sweetser, SJ

Dear Kate,

Thank you for all your strong support and encouragement with this project. Your insights on the Board are much appreciated.

Tom Sweetser
May, 2019

A Crossroad Book
The Crossroad Publishing Company
Chestnut Ridge, New York

The Crossroad Publishing Company
www.crossroadpublishing.com
© 2019 by Fr. Thomas J. Sweetser, SJ

In continuation of our 200-year tradition of independent publishing, The Crossroad Publishing Company proudly offers a variety of books with strong, original voices and diverse perspectives. The viewpoints expressed in our books are not necessarily those of The Crossroad Publishing Company, any of its imprints or of its employees, executives, owners. Although the author and publisher have made every effort to ensure that the information in this book was correct at press time, the author and publisher do not assume and hereby disclaim any liability to any party for any loss, damage, or disruption caused by errors or omissions, whether such errors or omissions result from negligence, accident, or any other cause. No claims are made or responsibility assumed for any health or other benefits.

Book design by the HK Scriptorium
Cover design by George Foster

Library of Congress Cataloging-in-Publication Data available from the Library of Congress.

ISBN: 978-0-8245-9966-9

Books published by The Crossroad Publishing Company may be purchased at special quantity discount rates for classes and institutional use. For information, please email sales@crossroadpublishing.com.

In memory of my brother,
Dr. Theodore H. Sweetser Jr.,
who kept the faith and
remained committed
to the Catholic Church
throughout his life

Contents

Acknowledgments

This book is the compilation of the reflections of those people who agreed to be interviewed. Without their insights and observations, this work would not have been produced.

Credit is due also to my former co-worker, Debora A. Elkins, who edited and corrected repeated versions of the manuscript. My thanks, as well, to my sister and brother-in-law, Kathleen and Richard Hage, for their support, and to my niece, Sara Sweetser, who offered help at a critical juncture.

A special thank you to Gwendolin Herder, publisher of The Crossroad Publishing Company, for her encouragement and willingness to accept this book for publication.

Foreword

It is no secret that more people are leaving the Catholic Church in the United States than entering it. Former Catholics now make up more than 10 percent of the U.S. population. Those who leave do so mostly as teenagers.

About half of those leaving become unchurched—the "nones"—while the other half become Protestants. Of those who become Protestant, most become Evangelicals, attracted by a welcoming community, vibrant services, and an emphasis on the Bible.

Pope Francis recognized the problem the Church has in communicating with young people. He held a synod of bishops to discuss the Church's outreach to the young in October of 2018. Earlier in March 2018, he held a presynod meeting with young people to get their thoughts.

Pope Francis helped the synodal fathers—yes, they were all men—understand the importance of listening to young people and accompanying them on their journey. Although they were not voting members of the synod, young people were present who spoke to the assembly and participated in discussion groups with the bishops.

One weakness of this youthful input was that all of the young people were devoted Catholics. Many of them even worked for the Church. As a result, the bishops did not hear from those who had given up on the Church and left.

Thomas Sweetser does not make that mistake. For this book, he interviewed fifty-five people of all ages and locations in the United States who were selected because they were pulling away from active involvement in the Church. He wanted to hear their stories about why that was so. Some of them were still Catholic (thirty-three) and others had moved out of the Church (twenty-two).

Originally, the author planned to publish this book in 2013, but the election of Pope Francis put the Church in an entirely different context so as to put his research into question. Rather than abandoning his project, he saw a new opportunity. He decided to go back to the same interviewees and find out if Pope Francis made a difference in their views of the Church.

The result is an extraordinary book that gives us one of the first in-depth studies of the impact of Pope Francis on those who were questioning their place in the Church. The reader gets to hear in their own words from those who have left and those who are on the margins. These are exactly the people who should have been at the synod on young people; these are the people to whom the bishops need to listen.

My own view is that although Francis is an extremely attractive promoter of the faith, he cannot do it alone. Too many people are inspired by Francis to give the Church a second chance but, when they return to their local parish, find not Francis but the same old attitudes that drove them away in the first place.

Until priests proclaim the same compassionate and loving Jesus that Francis does, until parishes are the welcoming field hospitals that Francis longs for, those returning will make a U-turn and leave the Church never to return.

The Church needs to listen to the voices in this book.

Thomas J. Reese, SJ
Senior Analyst
Religion News Service

An Energizing Church

> *My sheep were scattered,*
> *They wandered over all the mountains*
> *And on every high hill;*
> *My sheep were scattered*
> *Over all the face of the earth,*
> *With no one to search or seek for them.*
>
> Ezekiel 34:6

Mary Jo had been a highly active Catholic until she couldn't take it any longer. When interviewed in 2011 she remarked, "I struggled for about ten years to find a spiritual home within the Church, but I didn't find the hierarchical institution of the Catholic Church to be a place that nourishes, challenges, and supports me. The notion of justice articulated in Catholic social teaching is a core value for me, a value I came to as a result of my formation within the Church. But that same notion of justice, which makes the dignity, respect, and development of all human beings primary, does not seem to be a value within the institutional Church."

Another woman, **Theresa**, was in her early fifties when first interviewed in 2011. She left the Church at an early age. As she told it, "I was fourteen years old when I was at Mass, and an usher came up to me and said, 'Young lady, you can't wear those jeans in church. I'm afraid you will have to leave.' I went out of there and never went back. That experience changed my life, and my membership in the Catholic Church."

Arthur, at one time an involved parishioner, remarked, "I didn't leave the Church, the Church left me. By 'Church' I mean both locally and the hierarchy, what they say and what they do. Their principles and mine got farther and farther apart. I didn't hear much about sharing with others but more about doctrines and rules related to women's issues and sexuality."

These three experiences are but samples of what caused people to pull back from active involvement in the Church before Francis became the pope. Those who were accustomed to attending liturgy regularly began to let weekends slip by without coming to Mass. In most cases, they didn't feel guilty about it. Some of these took their nonattendance a step further by giving up on the Catholic Church altogether.

Trying to get a handle on what was happening in the Catholic Church in 2011 was tricky business. At this time, Pope Benedict XVI seemed to be emphasizing conformity to doctrine and moral imperatives, heading toward a leaner, more orthodox membership. This approach was in contrast with those who, rather than limiting the requirements for being part of the Church, wanted to keep the invitation open to all comers, stressing a more inclusive rather than exclusive approach. Fifty years earlier, the Second Vatican Council fostered a more open, interactive Church institution. By 2011, the voices seeking dialogue and compromise were fading into the background.

"This is not what Jesus intended," one less active Catholic complained in desperation. The result was that good and faithful Catholics began to give up the struggle and go elsewhere. Others did not. They planted their feet firmly within their faith communities and remained Catholic despite the turmoil and abuse they experienced.

One example was **Terry.** Both he and his wife continued to attend Mass but had pulled back from active involvement. "I am remaining because I am Catholic. Being Catholic is bigger than dogmas or doctrines. I fight for the 'little church' over against the 'bigger Church.' I am in the league with those who want the Church itself to move on."

Ed, a man who was in his seventies when first interviewed in 2011, withdrew from involvement in his parish and joined a community that saw itself as a prophetic witness to the larger institution. "Our faith community sees itself as essentially Catholic, albeit on a parallel track from the increasingly rigid, hierarchical Church that I find to be such a scandal. The hopes engendered by the reforms of Vatican Council II promised greater inclusion of the baptized in the life of the Church, less clerical controls, diminished centralized decision making and respect for action on behalf of justice for all, in short, increased servant leadership in the example of Jesus."

There was no doubt that many American Catholics were leaving and going elsewhere. Studies of Church membership showed this, as did the census figures from parishes across the nation. This was not a new phenomenon. People had been leaving the Church ever since Jesus invited people to "eat my body and drink my blood," in Chapter 6 of John's Gospel. People turned away then and no longer were counted among his disciples. What appeared different at the beginning of this century was the magnitude and suddenness of the shift.

For many individuals, this did not mean that they no longer consider themselves to be "Catholic" in many dimensions of their lives. It was part of their mindset. Nor had they stopped growing spiritually as they searched for meaning in their lives and where God fit in. If people had a chance to tell their stories of their faith journeys that led them out of the Catholic Church, perhaps this would provide clues as to what reforms or changes might be needed, especially on the local parish level.

There might also be important information obtained from stories of those who had decided to stay within the Catholic fold. What caused them difficulties and how did they cope with them? At one time they were fully active, not only coming regularly to

Mass but volunteering for ministries and leadership positions in their parish and in the larger Church. With the right environment and a sincere invitation, might they be open to returning to active involvement?

Gathering the Stories

With great hopes of discovering the feelings and motivations of those who were pulling back from active involvement in the Church and parish life, I set out to personally interview those who were withdrawing their support and participation in the Church, or who had decided to leave the Catholic Church entirely. Between May of 2011 and September of 2012, I interviewed fifty-five persons as a way of offering a small sampling of what people were feeling about the Catholic Church, both large scale and small. They ranged in age from twenty to over eighty. They were spread across the country, from Maryland to California, and represented the thoughts of both men and women. The criteria for being interviewed was that they had been actively involved in parish or institutional life but now were struggling with one or other aspect of the larger Church or local parish that caused them to be less committed.

Because of my involvement with Catholic parishes and groups throughout the United States for forty years, I was able to draw on a wealth of contacts to construct a list of those to be interviewed. When I mentioned this writing project to those I encountered in my travels, people would mention, "I would love to tell my story," or, "Oh, you should talk to this person." Many of those I interviewed led me to others, thus expanding the network of people to be included. Each person was assured anonymity.

Each person contacted was given a list of topics from which to choose in order to give a focus to their stories. The ones they chose were authority, sexuality, women's issues, liturgy, social justice, and spirituality. They were also asked whether they were remaining Catholic or were "moving on." Of the fifty-five people who were interviewed, twenty-two said they were on their way out of the Church and thirty-three indicated that they were remaining.

Many of those who chose to remain in the Church were patient, weathering many storms and struggles to remain faithful in the midst of turmoil. They "hung in there," seeking to change and renew the Church from within. "Despite the struggles, I have remained in the Church because I feel that I can effect more from *within* than from *outside* the Catholic system and structure," remarked **Ginny**, a woman in her mid-sixties.

For others, their patience had worn thin, and they were searching for other options and possibilities. The word "Catholic" still had meaning for them, but not as they had previously experienced it. **Theresa**, who left the Church at the age of fourteen, reflected, "To be honest, I think much would depend on which Catholic Church was next door to me. If it fit my needs and desires, I might begin to attend it again."

A Sudden Shift

In March of 2013, beyond all expectations, Jorge Mario Bergoglio, a Jesuit, was elected the new pope and took the name Francis. No Jesuit had ever been called to that office, and the name of Francis had never before been chosen. What was he like? What were his priorities? What changes would he make? No one knew the answers to these and many other questions. Everything was in flux.

His priorities and emphases were not what people were expecting. He did not fit into the mold of what a pope usually acted like. He washed the feet of a Muslim woman in prison; he chose to live in a simple apartment and not in the papal residence; he paid attention to the poor and made friends with ordinary people, not those in positions of authority or privilege. He stressed caring for those in need rather than strict observance of Church rules and regulations. Those he selected as cardinals were not from the typical countries or major cities. This was altogether new and exciting news for those seeking a shift in Church and papal authority.

The election of Pope Francis provided a new focus for the interviews obtained in 2011 and 2012. No longer was the question, "What kept some people in the Church and others to leave it?" Now it was, "Has the pope influenced people's attitudes and practices toward the Church since he was elected?" To give people time to shape their reaction to the new pope, on the advice of a Jesuit friend, I waited four years into Francis's papacy before attempting to locate the people I had originally interviewed.

The effort to find those I had talked with in 2011–2012 began in January of 2017. Of the original fifty-five, two had died and only one did not want to share her thoughts because of health difficulties. The remaining fifty-two were not only willing to be interviewed a second time but were happy, even excited, to share their experiences of the new pope. Between February and June of 2017, I was able to interview all fifty-two people. They were asked whether the pope had made a difference to them, whether he had changed their attitudes toward the Church or Church practices, what more they would like him to accomplish, and whether they felt the change of focus and direction he had initiated would continue after he was no longer the pope.

In the summer of 2018, another event occurred that affected the leadership and people alike. An American cardinal was removed from the College of Cardinals, and a report released by a grand jury in Pennsylvania concerning sexual abuse by priests and attempts by bishops to cover it up captured the headlines. The public reaction was significant enough to return for a third time to those interviewed in order to learn their feelings and desires regarding what changes they judged necessary and how the pope should respond to these events. Their responses are contained in Chapter 14.

Structure of the Book

The book is divided into two sections. The first one contains the reflections of both those who had left the Catholic Church and those who had remained at the time the original interviews took place in 2011–2012. It also contains suggestions both groups offered about what a parish could do to become more attentive and inviting to both its own members and those seeking a new spiritual home.

The second section offers insights into people's reactions to the pope, both those who had left the Church and those who remained. Chapter 10 contains the views of those who are no longer Catholic. Despite their positive impressions of the pope, only a few said they would consider taking a second look at returning to the Church. For most it was too late to make any changes. Chapter 11 includes the opinions of those who are remaining Catholic, although many still voiced difficulties with one or other aspect of the larger Church institution or the local parish scene. One area that did trigger strong feelings from both those within and those on the outside was the role of women in the Church. This is the subject of Chapter 12. There is also the question of Francis's influence on parish life and leadership. Chapter 13 covers these responses.

In order to put the comments from those interviewed into context, it is important at the outset to take a look at the wider scope of the Catholic Church in the United States prior to the election of Pope Francis in March of 2013.

How People Felt about the Church prior to Francis Becoming the Pope

You do not feed the sheep.
You have not strengthened the weak,
You have not brought back the strayed,
You have not sought the lost,
But with force and harshness
You have ruled them.

Ezekiel 34:3-4

Chapter 1

The Degree of the Problem

"Look around the church," one active parishioner mentioned. "What do you see? Empty pews, gray heads, and few young people. Where is everyone?"

"Our collection is down," a pastor remarked. "Fewer people are giving. Thank goodness our active parishioners are giving more or we would be in real trouble."

Are there fewer Catholics? Are more people leaving than joining? The answer in 2011 was both yes and no. Much depended on geography and ethnicity. Although the greatest number of Catholics still lived in the Northeastern part of the United States, the numbers were growing in the South and Southwest, primarily because of the movement from the Rust Belt to the Sun Belt and because of the influx of Hispanic Catholics. Some were immigrants; others had been in the country for some time and tended to have larger families than non-Hispanic Catholics. This complicated the issue.

Yes, there was a drop in the number who were baptized as infants but who no longer called themselves Catholic. The Pew Religious Landscape Survey conducted in 2007 uncovered 32 percent who fit this category. Some of this loss was offset by converts joining the Church later in life. The Landscape Survey put this number at 24.5 percent. This resulted in a net loss of 7.5 percent once the converts were subtracted from those who were Catholics from birth but later left the Church.

Another factor, however, neutralized this loss. This was the influx of immigrants to the United States, many of whom were of Hispanic lineage and belonged to the Catholic faith. This addition kept the percentage of Catholics in the United States in 2007 at around 24 percent.

As a result of these trends, a parish in the Northeast or Midwest might experience a noticeable drop in attendance because of population shifts in the area, the retired moving south, younger people looking for jobs elsewhere, a less significant influx of Hispanics, and couples having fewer children than in years past so there are not as many young people as a whole.

One example of this shift was in the Youngstown, Ohio, Diocese. In 2010 there were 118 parishes, but by 2012, there were 80, a result of downsizing through closures, consolidations, and clustering. Not only were there not enough priests to staff the parishes, there were not enough parishioners to keep the parishes viable.

Head to a parish in the South or West, however, and one found a different story. Saint Michael the Archangel, a parish in a suburb of Denver, Colorado, had five Masses on the weekend, four in English and one in Spanish. Because of the good music, insightful preaching, a prayerful atmosphere, and close community, the number count for the English liturgies held steady, while the one Mass in Spanish was bursting at the seams. Those in charge of that liturgy clamored for a second Mass in Spanish. There did not seem to be a drop in the Catholics attending that parish; just the opposite.

What about the 32 percent of those raised Catholic who decided to leave the Church and either join another faith or go it alone? The Pew Landmark Survey provided information about why they left. A large number of people were surveyed—35,000 adults, 10,545 of whom identified themselves as presently or at one time members of the Catholic Church. Of the 32 percent who had left the Church, 18 percent joined another religion, either a mainline Protestant faith (6%), an Evangelical church (9%), or some other religion (3%). Fourteen percent (14%) had not joined any other faith; they remained unaffiliated and on their own.

For the 18 percent who had joined another church or religious group, a frequently mentioned reason for making this choice was that their spiritual needs were not being met in the Catholic Church or by a local parish. Seventy-one percent (71%) felt this contributed to their decision to leave the Church. Seventy percent (70%) said they found the church or religion they joined to be more appealing than the Catholic faith.

For those who left but did not join another faith, many of them (65%) stopped believing in what the Catholic Church taught, especially in the areas of sexuality, such as abortion, homosexuality, and contraception.

The clergy sexual abuse scandal was not a prominent reason for leaving the Catholic Church for either those joining other faiths (21%) or those who remained unaffiliated (27%). Although not a significant determinant, it did help to confirm their decision; many at that time lost faith in the leadership of the Catholic Church.

One significant finding from the Landscape Survey results was not about *why* people had left the Catholic Church, but *when*. At what age did people make a decision to look elsewhere? For most, it was at a young age. Of the 14 percent who left the Church and remained unaffiliated with any other religion, close to half (48%) did so before they reached the age of nineteen, and another 30 percent did so before they became twenty-four. Only 22 percent of the unaffiliated left the Church later in life, twenty-four years of age or older.

What was not included in these statistics was the loss of those who had been active in the Church and local parish for many years. The level of frustration and discontent by many of these involved Catholics had reached the point where they made the choice to leave the Church. Cathleen Kaveny wrote an article in *Commonweal* entitled, "Long Goodbye: Why Some Devout Catholics Are Leaving the Church" (*Commonweal*, October 22, 2010, p. 8). In that article she listed a number of reasons why good and faithful Catholics were making this choice.

- God's saving grace is everywhere, not merely within the structure of the Roman Catholic Church, so they believe that they will remain within Christ's church, even as they loosen their ties with the Catholic communion.
- The Catholic Church is not acting like Christ's church now, especially regarding teachings on matters of sexual morality (contraception and gay marriage, for instance) or gender roles (the all-male priesthood).
- Not being able to trust the good sense and good faith of Church leadership, not being confident in the present trajectory of the post-Vatican II Church, especially regarding ecumenism, collegiality, and the role of the laity.
- The poor handling by the hierarchy of the sexual-abuse crisis, which undermined the bishops' claim to wisdom on difficult and divisive issues of sexual ethics.
- Seeing no hope of institutional reform but, instead, calling for loyal deference to ecclesiastical authority in all matters.
- That remaining in the Catholic Church appears to be futile and perhaps includes complicity with evil.
- Not liking what remaining in the Church is doing to them, including the diminishment of their ability to hear the Gospel, to proclaim that Good News, and experience the peace of Christ.

In 2012, the Diocese of Trenton, NJ, asked Fr. William J. Byron, SJ, of St. Joseph University, and Dr. Charles Zech, of Villanova University, to conduct an online survey to learn why some Catholics had left the Church. (See "Why They Left: Exit Interviews Shed Light on Empty Pews," *America Magazine*, April 30, 2012.) Some of the reasons mentioned included the following:

- Doctrinal concerns, including the exclusion of women from ordination, the perception that persons of homosexual orientation were unwelcome, the complexity of the annulment process, the barring of divorced and remarried persons from the sacraments.

- Not having a good explanation of the Eucharist, along with more creative pastoral liturgies, interactive music that encouraged involvement, and preaching that inspired and challenged people's values.

- Fewer priests who are approachable and do not appear arrogant, distant, unavailable, uncaring, or who are hard to understand because of their accent.

- No matter the size of the parish, the need for a welcoming, caring community so that no one feels alone or lost in the crowd.

Chapter 2

Reactions from Those Who Had Moved On

Of the fifty-five people originally interviewed in 2011–2012, twenty-three (42%) fit the category of "moving on." Nine of them were men and fourteen women. All but three were baptized as infants and grew up in the Catholic faith. Most were, at one time, very active members of the parish. All had, at one time, regularly attended Mass. The ages ranged from young to old. Four were in their twenties or early thirties, five were in their late thirties or forties, nine were in their fifties to early sixties, and five were sixty-five years of age or older. Two of the twenty-three mentioned that they were gay.

In preparation for the interview, people were asked to choose a topic as a way of focusing their reflections. Six picked *authority* as their issue, eight chose *justice*, which included *women's issues*, four settled on *sexuality*, and four centered on *spirituality*. There was, in other words, a broad spectrum of concerns and interests among those being interviewed.

Authority

Those who chose authority had trouble with its misuse by the hierarchy, and at times by the local pastor. **Bob**, a gentleman in his seventies at the time, explained why he chose authority as a focus. "Top-down authority is the overall tenor of the Church.

Everything else stems from that, whether it be sexuality, secrecy, whatever the issue; it all comes back to this approach to authority. The world is moving toward a bottom-up authority not a top-down one, yet the Church is just the opposite. Everything that turns me off about the Church comes from this approach."

Mike, a young man in his late thirties, was at one time very active in his parish, eventually becoming the chair of the pastoral council. He explained why he chose the topic of Church authority. "When I was in college, the local bishop was heavy-handed in taking the Church back to more traditional ways. He allowed no discussion and no questioning of what he said. It was just something to be received by the faithful. According to him, the priest is to be the *persona Christi*, which means that 'I'm the person of Jesus Christ to you.' It puts priests up on a pedestal. This way of thinking and acting didn't go down very well, especially in reaction to the sex abuse issue and how it was handled by the bishops. I just didn't believe the hierarchy any more. From that moment on the bishops had to earn their authority, and most bishops didn't see the need to do that."

Peggy, a former nun and now the mother of two grown children, remarked, "Authority was the biggest thing I faced when I decided not to remain in the Church. This is where the main problem is. Not every member of the hierarchy is the problem. But the collective voice of the hierarchy is the issue. There are some good bishops and archbishops in dioceses and I can appreciate that. But the problem is—and it has taken me years to figure this out—taken as a whole, they are bullies."

Once a faithful parish participant, **Arthur,** at the time of the first interview in 2011, was on the fringes of Church involvement. "I have no faith in the hierarchy who set the rules and enforce them. They are unlike Christ."

The story of **Mary Jo** had much to do with rules and regulations. She grew up Catholic and from a young age had been active in her local parish. "I never really evaluated what I was hearing from the Church and the hierarchy, whether it was just or not. I never questioned this, even when I was raising my own children. I blindly accepted what I was taught and what I experienced within the Church.

"The first thing that was unjust enough for me to start questioning it was the Church's pedophile crisis. The abuse of children by priests, over the course of time, changed me. I first gave the bishops the benefit of the doubt. I couldn't grasp the notion that the hierarchy would so blatantly ignore the Church's social teachings and the commandments of God. But I came to see that the only thing that was important to the bishops was maintaining power, wealth, and image.

"As I became aware of this, that the bishops were not responding justly, I began to question whether the institutional Church was the place where I could find what I needed. I would go to church and would be arguing in my head with the leaders of the Church, that they were saying one thing but were doing another.

"I initially tried to change things from within the Church, feeling that change was necessary. I discovered there were many people in my parish community who weren't interested in pursuing the social teachings of our faith. They felt they were good Catholics if they went to church every week, were against the big moral issues of abortion and homosexual activity. I was uncomfortable in this environment.

"Conversations with my children helped me make the decision to leave. One concrete issue pushed me over the edge—not hiring an actively gay person, although the person was the best qualified. This decision was based on a fear of losing money, not on social teachings or the Gospel. I couldn't be honest with myself when this happened.

"The hierarchy's response to sexual abuse and women's issues frustrated me, but so did the attitudes of the Catholics around me who were content to take on a few issues but were not willing to confront the more challenging ones. It is not enough to be against abortion; we also have to be willing to support a mother who gives birth but can't afford to care for her child, or speak out against the killing of innocent babies in Iraq. It's easy for a person to say publicly, 'I'm against birth control,' but then go ahead and use birth control privately. Or to say, 'I want to send my child to a Catholic school,' but will not support an undocumented family that also wants Catholic schooling for the children. The Catholic Church should be in the middle of this struggle over immigration. It's not just the hierarchy; it's many of the well-off Catholic laity as well."

Mark was a searching, inquisitive young man in his twenties who studied theology in a Catholic college and learned to ask questions. At the time of the interview, he was teetering on the edge. As he put it, "I am leaning more and more toward leaving the Church and moving on. I haven't been to Mass for a long time; this is not where my energy lies. I have many concerns, especially those connected with sexual ethics and gender. These are the big ones for me. When I try to engage the Church in dialogue, the response I hear is, 'That is just too bad you feel this way but there is nothing to talk about.' At some point I had to ask myself, 'What is the point of sticking around and trying to push the Church toward being more Christian?' This is just being complicit with the injustices I see in the Church. Change is unlikely so it is better that I do what I can from outside the structure. The small part I can contribute to reform is not recognized by those in authority in the Church. The only way I see to challenge this type of power is to remove myself from recognizing any validity it has over my faith life."

A number of those interviewed made the distinction between their parish and what they experienced from the hierarchy. Mike, who earlier talked about being in college and finding the bishop heavy-handed, said, "Eventually, I came to feel that I was being called out of the Church, and as time went on this call became stronger. When I realized that this was a true calling not to be Catholic it was a shock to me. I've been a Catholic my whole life; it is such a part of my identity. This new realization was heart-wrenching. I love my parish, the people, and the current pastor. If it wasn't for this place where I worship, I would have left a long time ago. I became involved in this parish as a result of meeting the pastor in his previous assignment. When he was changed he sent me a letter from his new parish asking me to come join this community. And so I did. I discovered a community that was very supportive of one another. It's a small place so it is hard not to become involved. I was an outreach minister at first, then a lector, then participated in religious formation and finally was elected to serve on the pastoral council.

"But now I have to listen to what my gut is saying. It is telling me to go, but I don't know where to go. I've tried to remain loyal to the institution, but I don't think I can do that any more. So I'm going to start church shopping. There is always the possibility that I will come back to the Catholic Church, but for now I need to move on. I am very disheartened by the direction in which the Church is heading, and I feel alienated from the institution. I now feel like the lines around what is acceptably Catholic (perhaps orthodox is a better word) have been so narrowly drawn that I am excluded by it.

"What is hard about this is that I have always had a church base, and now I am letting go of that. This is very difficult. My anchor has been my local parish. I still have friends there—they are so understanding. Others are not as supportive; they try to talk me out of it. To me this is a crisis of denomination, not a crisis of faith.

"I left the Church because I could no longer attend the Eucharistic celebration. To me the celebrant, that is, the priest, has to embody the Spirit of Christ and the Church. If the celebrants believe the Church has the right to bully people and totally negate their lives within the Church, how can they—the celebrants—represent Christ? The authorities of the Church should stand up for what is good and noble and honest. But instead, they have hid behind their authority to cover their own reputations, contending that 'the Church is perfect and pure.' As a result, they have to cover up the actions of pedophile clerics."

Justice

Closely linked to Church authority is the issue of justice. **Christina**, a woman who was in her forties when first interviewed, grew up in an atmosphere of Catholic social teachings, which she receive both from her parents and from the Catholic schools she attended. What caused her to leave the Catholic Church? Here is her explanation:

"I developed my sense of justice and equality through the Church. Yet, I have become discouraged by the Church's lack of direct action to create a more just and equitable Church community and society. Racism, sexism, classism, and other 'isms' persist, with very little acknowledgment or call to action from the Church. Male domination within the Church, the lack of recognition of sexism, racism, and white privilege deeply anger and frustrate me. Instead of being a force for change, the Church helps to keep systems of inequity, injustice, and privilege in place. I deeply appreciate my Catholic heritage and upbringing, and I feel very much at home with Catholics. I hope to return to the Church when there is more space for justice work.

"I don't expect perfection, but the contradictions I saw in the institutional Church got to be too harsh and extreme. They came out against gays and women and concentrated on wealth and power instead. I came to realize that to be part of the Church meant that I was part of the problem instead of part of the solution. I could no longer be associated with this repressive institution. I choose instead to stand by my gay and African American friends.

"Those seeking change are slammed down by Church leaders. When a parish community becomes too progressive, a conservative pastor is appointed, and once again, those seeking change are 'slammed down.' These types of controls prevent people from carrying out the teachings of the Gospels. It is a dangerous environment to take any action that threatens the authorities and their pronouncements. The Church does not support those acting for the poor or becoming agents for change. Yet it is hopeful that there are still people in the Church standing up for change."

One of the pressing issues raised in the 2011 interviews was the treatment of women in the Catholic Church. **Susie** and **Charlie**, a married couple in their fifties, spoke eloquently on the subject.

"We have both been raised Catholic and were very active in the local Catholic parish. It is easy to say we have had every position available to laity at our parish. But as time went on, the 'table' was less and less welcoming to women. That has been at the insistence of the hierarchy, and that is why we had to leave. We did not want to become bitter.

"We have been waiting since Vatican II for more change, and it has not come. In fact, it feels as if it is going backward. We came to the conclusion that the Catholic Church can't get it right until they admit women to the highest levels of decision making, not just to ordination. In companies where women have been involved at the highest level of decision making, for example, on the boards of highly successful mutual funds, the research bears out that these companies do better than companies that still run on the 'old boys' system. We do better when the table is more inclusive! All of humanity needs to be involved. It will happen! But we do not believe it will happen in our lifetime.

"It appears that the hopes of Vatican II and the loving kindness of so many church leaders has been 'put under a bushel' by the Church. Without all of God's people at the decision-making table of the Lord, we are all in the dark. We seek a place to shine with and among all. For that reason we have moved on to membership in the Unitarian Church. The church we attend now is 60 percent former Catholics. We're not losing our background; we are continuing the search for our path, for community.

Bridget, a woman who was in her forties at the time of the first interview, put it in more personal terms. "My gender was the reason the Catholic Church denied me the opportunity to heed my call, to follow my vocation. In my head and heart, I know myself to be both competent and equal to men, and yet the Catholic Church categorically denies me that reality. The Catholic Church says women can only do certain things, such as offering a reflection, leading a Communion service, visiting the sick, because, in an ancillary way, these ministries belong to the role of priesthood. The church I am serving now—not a Catholic parish—sought out and celebrated my gifts. I'm a minister in a faith community that actively wanted a female to balance the ministry of their male pastor.

"At the Catholic college where I studied, one of my priest teachers and I went round and round over coffee, discussing my vocation. This is when I began to articulate my inner truth of being wholly competent. The priest told me, 'Damn it, Bridget, you're going to change the Church from the inside or from the outside. You decide which one!' And so for years I worked from the grassroots for change within. I wanted to help thinking Catholics find ways to live happy, healthy, holy, faith-filled lives. The pastor at the parish where I was a lay ecclesial minister said to me when I decided to move on, 'I am sad for the Catholic Church, but so happy for you.'

"I had no idea what the reaction from my family would be when I decided to leave the Catholic Church. Family was the reason I stayed a Catholic for as long as I did. I was raised in a very devout, Irish-Catholic family, not just church-going, but culturally Catholic as well. I was deeply imbedded in the culture and myth of my ancestors who came to this country under great oppression and stress. Catholic loyalty and steadfastness were parts of my ancestry that connected me to my family. What would my parents say to me when I told them I was taking a position in a Protestant church where I was seeking ordination? My dad's comment was, 'You know this has been inevitable since you went to study at the Catholic seminary.' What I wanted to reply, but didn't, was, 'Actually, Daddy, it has been inevitable since you had me baptized.'"

Connie, a woman who was in her fifties, described how the Church's attitude toward women colored her entire religious experience, beginning from an early age. "I was young when Vatican II was going on, and so many new things were happening, except for the role of women in the Church. I thought, 'What's wrong with us women?' I am a mover and a questioner, and this was a big question for me. I felt left out. As a woman I wasn't as important and couldn't do lots of things that the men could do. I did not feel whole, and that Jesus felt differently about me than about men.

"I went to Catholic schools when growing up. I can remember being frustrated that I could help the nuns clean the church in the summertime—and it was a great time for me—but that was as far as we women could go.

"After I got married and was raising a family, my oldest daughter wanted to be an altar server, but our pastor would not let her do this. She was very disappointed, and I was angry about it. I talked with our pastor, asking why she couldn't do this. Some other parishes were beginning to allow this. He said that the bishop didn't want it. Ten years later, when my youngest daughter was in third or fourth grade, she was able to be an altar server.

"I served on different boards and committees in our parish—I was very active. The women did the bulk of the work in the parish, but I thought we were always second class. Spiritually this is not how things should be. The Bible was written in patriarchal times so women were not equal back then as well. Now I realize that it is really a control issue, not a spiritual issue. It is not the way it is supposed to be. I moved on because of this patriarchal attitude in the Catholic Church.

"Back when I was still Catholic, there was a time I could talk with our pastor. I could be easy with him—I could ask a lot of questions. I even helped him get into sobriety. I would be glad to tell those in my old parish or someone in the Catholic Church about my present faith belief, but I've not been asked by anyone, except my mom and she is great with it!"

Sexuality

This was an important topic for most of the young people interviewed in 2011–2012. Church regulations and approaches toward sexual morality caused those in their twenties much anger and turmoil, resulting in a change in their religious affiliation. In 2011, **Rafael** was a young Hispanic gay man who graduated from a Catholic university shortly before our original conversation. He told of his struggles at an early age with Church mandates. "I was born and raised Catholic in Mexico, having received all of the initiation sacraments of baptism, first communion, confession, and confirmation. It was my mom who took me to church, and I went to a Catholic high school and university. When I was fourteen years of age, I spoke to a priest, asking him about being gay. His response was that it was not wrong to be gay, but acting it out was wrong. I haven't been part of the Church since that moment.

"The Church's attitude toward contraceptives is irresponsible, especially in a world with almost seven billion people and with such large health crises related to sexually transmitted diseases. The stance on homosexuality is also contradictory, that is, being gay is not wrong but having gay relations is. These two are the main issues I have with the Catholic Church regarding sexuality.

"It has been a long time since I have been part of the Catholic Church because I didn't feel welcomed there. I felt my very identity was being threatened by the policies of the Church, and I don't want to be any part of that. Religion of any kind is not something I can get into anymore. When I talked with my mom after speaking with that priest as a young teenager, she stuck to the Church's position as well. What I liked about the Catholic Church is that it is more tradition based than Bible based, and for the Church, the Bible is not literally true as it is in other religions. My problems with the Church lie elsewhere. Now I am more of a naturalist; I don't believe in God."

Jonathan, another young gay person, had a similar reaction. "Sexuality is the most glaring reason for wanting to leave the Catholic Church. I'm gay, and because of that, I don't feel welcomed by the larger, institutional Church. There are also the issues of birth control and how women are treated.

"I was baptized Catholic from birth. My mother was a convert and my father was not a Catholic, so I didn't have a strong Catholic background as I was growing up. Both my brother and I stopped attending church when we were young, right around the time that the sex abuse issue surfaced in the Church.

"When I attended a Jesuit university I began to become more active as a Catholic. The school was much more open to gays; there were gay associations on campus, and faculty members spoke out about rights for gay people. Because of this experience, I felt that Church on the local level was great, but not on the larger scale.

"I have little hope for change within the Church, and I'm not waiting around for this to happen any time soon. It's a psychological thing for me. I need to find a more fulfilling and less oppressive experience of Church in a different environment. There are gay-friendly groups on the local level in various parishes, but statements coming from the larger Church condemn my civil rights. I am ashamed by this and want no part of it. So I'm searching for another church, perhaps becoming Episcopalian, where there are women in leadership positions and an openness to gay rights and marriage. It is hopeless to expect such changes from the top of the Catholic Church structure."

Fanny, also in her twenties and born in Mexico, lamented the stance of the Catholic Church regarding sexual ethics. "I don't think anyone can control my life, my body, and my reproductive rights. The top officials in the Church are all men. They don't understand. We need women leaders as well. It will be better if women were included. As it is now, the Church leadership does not make good decisions about women. As long as there is inequality regarding women I can't be part of it. The Church does have social justice as an ideal, but the hierarchy is not putting this ideal into practice.

"By sophomore year of college it was no more Church for me. Before that I felt a lot of stress regarding sexuality. I didn't feel comfortable identifying with being a Catholic because of the suffering the Church's rules caused me and others. I didn't want to be part of that. Now I am at peace."

The Church's stance on sexuality was not only an issue for young people. Colleen, a woman who was in her fifties when the first interview took place, picked this as the reason she no longer called herself a Catholic. As she explained, it, "I had been raised a Catholic and was involved in our local parish because it was someplace I felt I fit. The place where I belonged challenged us to question our lives but not judge those sitting next to us. At one time the Church was more welcoming and tolerant of differing ideas. The parish was a nurturing community that acknowledged the often bewildering journey of everyday life and gave me the sense that I was supported by the flock; we were in this together.

"The politics of the parish changed dramatically with a change in pastor. It was clear, once he arrived, that we were not encouraged to ask questions. Pamphlets were handed out at election time to instruct Catholics on how they must vote. It was a one-issue campaign. And my unwelcome question was, 'What about *other* social issues?'

"I felt a self-righteousness come over the parish. In areas of social justice, for instance, there was a blatant intolerance of same-sex marriage. For myself, I don't view the world with such a harsh judgment of others. The longer I stayed sitting in the pew, the more hypocritical I felt. My belief was that the Church should expand the privilege of marriage, support love and commitment and not promote disdain and hate.

"My involvement in the parish had been quite extensive, including being a Eucharistic minister, which I loved. It broke my heart when I was instructed to refuse communion to people we knew to be living together. That's not okay; I would not judge others.

"I realized then that *it was not okay to stay.* I was feeling more and more hypocritical sitting in church each week. My thoughts were often, 'I really do not think that Jesus would be judging like this!' I was leaving Mass frustrated, angry, and no longer feeling like I belonged. I came to realize that the Church was less interested in reaching out to people and was becoming more conservative, increasingly consumed with its superiority, exclusivity, and self-righteousness. These changes were not working for me; I was feeling out of place and decided to leave.

"There are some things that keep me connected to the church community, like when I hear about a parish family in need. Those are things I don't want to be cut off from. But I keep a distance. There is a piece of me that doesn't want to jump right back in. I can't. Yet there remains a piece of me, such as the desire to join others in reaching out to those in pain, which reminds me that a part of who I am is still Catholic. Maybe I need to find a new community outside formal religion for now."

Spirituality

As was mentioned in the previous chapter, the Pew Religious Landscape Survey of 2007 revealed that one of the primary reasons people left the Catholic Church to join a Protestant faith, either mainline or evangelical, was that their spiritual needs were not being met. Some of the interviews reinforced this perception.

Andrew, a man who was in his fifties when first we met, put the blame on the new pastor in the parish where he was highly engaged. "Spirituality is one of the biggest losses in the Church. It seems we are going back to a pre-Vatican II era, and I have become more and more disconnected and disillusioned about the Church. I was already struggling with the Church when our new pastor was assigned; he is quite arrogant. When he came he undid a parish that was doing so well. It was drawing people from all over the area and bringing back those who had left the Church. They were being spiritually nourished. People were encouraged to give their input, especially about what would encourage more people to become active in the parish. The new pastor didn't care about any of this. Our previous pastor, who was so good, was falsely accused of sexual abuse. He was open about it to the parishioners and they stood by him. He was eventually exonerated. We were a community supporting one another, pastor included.

"That all changed with the transition to a new pastor. My wife and I have left the parish and the Church recently. We could return someday, I suppose, but for now we are getting our needs met in a nondenominational church."

Theresa, who was mentioned in the Introduction as walking out of Mass and the Church as a teenager because an usher did not approve of her attire, picked spirituality as the focus for her interview. She picked this because, as she said, "This is what is most important to me. I myself have never been angry with the Catholic Church. I was more self-righteous about my beliefs when I was younger. Now I realize that all of the religions are so similar. I have a hard time putting boundaries around being in a particular religion; I can be part of each one. All of it appeals to me and can touch me. The best meditation I ever had was during a yoga class where I experienced the presence of Jesus. I felt I was loved at that moment."

Natalie, a well-educated former teacher who was over the age of sixty-five at the time of the first interview, also chose spirituality as a topic that piqued her interest. She explained, "I was fully involved in my parish, over the years a member of most every council and committee, always involved in community life, excited to visit our homebound with the Eucharist. Then everything changed. With our new priests, only they can touch the Eucharist. I am nothing now. I am to sit in the pew and totally respect the cassock that walks by, yet hear rebuke after rebuke of how unworthy, how evil, I am. I can't abide that.

"Going to church now leaves me angry and frustrated. I am not interested in joining another church or parish, although I know we all worship the same God. I don't know where I am moving to but I know I am moving away from this parish. I blame the Church and I blame the bishop for this.

"I have to feed my soul continually, and that can't happen in our parish or the Church the way it is now. The sexual abuse scandal is unreal. It seems to be unraveling more and more. The Church is not walking the walk and that hurts. The Church is no longer my universal connector as it once was.

"What I miss the most, as do all others I've talked with, is the community we once had. There is no more talking with each other after church as we once did, no more discussion about the homily, excitement about the next project, about the new school year. There is distrust; Catholics stare at one another with that look of being against other Catholics now—it's like the Inquisition. As a result, I am going elsewhere for my spirituality, going elsewhere to seek my Creator."

Finally, there is **Sally,** who was fifty years old in 2011 and never a Catholic. She was all set to join, but an experience with one of her children forced her to reconsider. Along with her husband, a life-long Catholic, she gave up on the Church. As she put it, "The main reason we chose to move was the stifling rules that seemed to bring down my children, rather than encourage their spiritual growth." She and her family joined the Episcopal Church where, as she said, "I felt accepted and was welcomed to participate fully in receiving communion. It was close enough to the Roman Catholic Church that my husband felt comfortable, but different enough that I was more at ease. The priest there was a woman and was allowed to follow the calling to preach, unlike in the Catholic Church."

Sources of Discontent

The four topics of authority, justice, sexuality, and spirituality are closely related. A common source of discontent was a leadership style and an exercise of authority that those interviewed experienced as top-down, secretive, and open to little or no consultation or dialogue. These stories came from intelligent, well-read, thinking lay members of the Church. When they discovered a bishop, or more likely, a pastor who listened and was sensitive to concrete needs and put pastoral concerns before rigid application of rules and regulations, they gave the person in authority the benefit of the doubt. They believed them to be honest and caring Church leaders and gave them their trust and support.

The reason these once-active Catholics went elsewhere was because they had lost faith in the collective voice of the hierarchy regarding issues and concerns that meant something to them personally. This is where all four topics come together. Authority, many felt, was being exercised with too narrow an orthodoxy that went against their understanding of Jesus Christ as portrayed in the Scriptures. As **Mike** mentioned earlier in the chapter, "this is a crisis of denomination, not a crisis of faith."

For others, the inappropriate exercise of authority was a justice issue. When the hierarchy operates from a position of absolute power, with no built-in structures of accountability, this leads to unjust behaviors, poor decision making, and the abuse of privilege. The sexual-abuse issue is one example of injustice cited by those interviewed. They saw it as a double standard, the bishops removing the abusers but taking little or no ownership themselves for their own share in the problem.

Both justice and sexuality issues came into play for those "moving on" when they considered how Church leaders dealt with both women and gays. Those interviewed experienced a rhetoric from "above" that was supposed to be accepting and welcoming, but in reality was often harsh and unforgiving. The response from these once-faithful but disenchanted Catholics was to no longer be associated with what they saw as a repressive institution. As one person put it, "It's a dangerous environment," and another saw it as "going backward."

How spirituality fits into the other topics is that many considered the way the Catholic Church operated was a detriment to their own spiritual growth, to their prayer life and their personal search for God. Their spirituality contained a set of core values that they felt were in jeopardy if they remained Catholic. For them, authentic spirituality included the following:

- Being able to lead a life of integrity and honesty that provides peace of mind rather than having to react against the fears, bullying, and duplicity they encountered in their experience of the Church.
- Fostering an inclusive atmosphere where all are welcomed and treasured in the parish and the Church for what they could offer to the community, both large and small.
- Emphasizing social justice stances that protected the rights of the poor and disadvantaged, and that put just practices into play, both within and outside of the parish and larger Church.
- Having the freedom to share their experiences and to speak openly about what they held dear, knowing that not all would agree with them. This openness comes from a culture of dialogue and shared seeking for what God is revealing to the community through the hopes and desires of those present.

Those interviewed didn't expect the Church to be perfect, but they did expect some movement in the direction of their hopes and aspirations. They did not find much evidence of this movement from those making the decisions. As a result, they were searching for some other way of being true to their values and dreams. Some found it in other churches and faith communities. Others continued searching. A few mentioned a willingness to return to full communion in the Catholic Church at some time in the future. As **Theresa** stated at the end of her sharing, "If it [the local parish] fit my needs and desires, I might begin to attend again."

Chapter 3

Still Growing Spiritually

The Scope of Spirituality

Although people may have left the Catholic Church, that does not mean that they had stopped their search for God or their efforts to discover what God had in store for them. The stories from those who had moved on were filled with accounts of discovering new ways of encountering the Sacred in their lives and taking their religious practices in a new direction. **Peggy,** a woman who was in her fifties when first interviewed in 2011, was once a religious sister. She left the order and by the time of the first interview had a grown family. She described her spiritual quest this way. "People hunger for spirituality, but the authorities, that is, the hierarchy of the Church, put limits on what is acceptable for the people. Spirituality is the relationship of individuals to their God, and holiness is what you do with your spirituality, that is, put it into action. Others see your good works, your holiness, and this comes from your spirituality."

Arthur, who was seventy years old and at one time an active Catholic, agreed that spirituality is about doing good for others. He no longer attended church, but he was still striving to carry out the mandates of the Gospel. "Christ's example was one of sharing, looking for the common good for everyone, being humble and caring for the least of the brethren. The basic principle for me is, 'Do unto others as you would have them do unto you.' My view of the Gospels is this preemptive message and Christ's instruction to live out this principle. All of the parables are about sharing with others—the multiplication of the loaves, the wedding feast at Cana, and multiple other examples of being inclusive of people and sharing what we have with others. The phrase of J. F. Kennedy in his inaugural address impressed me: 'Ask not what the country can do for you but what you can do for your country.' Also, when in college, there was a Center for Social Justice that had students going to Peru to do service projects during the summer. That helped lead me to my career in social service."

Theresa described spirituality this way: "It sounds trite, but I often ask myself, 'What would Jesus do.' I can't explain what is the criterion that I'm applying in order to answer this question, but it is always based on love.

"Recently I walked into church on Good Friday, and people were praying the rosary over and over again. It was meditative and spiritual. I have the same experience when I hear chanting in yoga or the ringing of bells in Mass. They are calling out to God. But this did not work for me when I was a kid. In the Church I felt like I needed to fight what was wrong with it. But outside the Church I was free to observe the beauty of nature or look in the eyes of someone I love and see God. Today, with all my spiritual journeys, I could probably come back to the Catholic Church and enjoy it. Of course, I would be ignoring some of the beliefs and rules I disagree with and would be there for the community, for the songs, for the joy of worship and service.

"My upbringing encouraged questioning and searching for the essentials. My parents were open to any beliefs we wished to have. It was okay to take the Bible and interpret it differently than others did. They taught us love above all, but also a strong sense of hope and that everything would turn out okay and that it was all for the good. And it is *all good*."

Natalie, a retired teacher at the time, continued her quest for a deeper spirituality, but had not found her parish or the Catholic

Church very helpful in this search. "My idea of spirituality is that it is a manifestation of the universal connection of the Creator with everyone and in all creation. Spirituality represented by the Catholic Church today is not what I need, although before our parish was sent its current pastor, I thought I was on the right path. I want spirituality to expand, not contract, my view of the Almighty, what we are about, and the why of creation. We are all to become the carriers of Christ's teachings. He said we are 'to care for one another as I have cared for you.' I will continue elsewhere to seek the universal connection I believe my Creator intended."

Fanny, a young Hispanic mother in her twenties, was raised Catholic. At the time of the first interview she no longer felt the need for spiritual guidance. "I never needed an intermediary between me and God. I am not an atheist. I believe Something is out there, but I don't have the answer as to what. How do I communicate with this Being? In nature, by being a happy parent, when I feel fully alive. Also when I go through hard times.

"But I don't like the institution telling me what to think. I can communicate with this Being and am grateful for that. I came to realize that the Church was not an effective way for me to communicate with God. The Church is not always helping people but is often just looking out for itself. I respect others who use the institution to help those in need, but some use it for the wrong reasons."

Community as Spiritually Enriching

Mary Jo was once a very active Catholic, but when interviewed she was on a different journey. She acknowledged the help she had received from her past and was working hard to maintain meaningful relationships in her life. "I had the opportunity to continue my education and spiritual formation through the Spiritual Exercises of St. Ignatius. I now look forward to exploring other options to nourish my spirituality and be part of new faith-sharing communities. How does it feel to be leaving the Church? Both just fine and not so good, all wrapped up together. I can never give up my Catholic identity—it's too much of who I am. I have grown close to the people in my parish community; that has been a large part of my life. If I don't go to Mass anymore, I won't see these people. My relationship with them changes. I have to figure out how to maintain these friendships without attending Mass, parish meetings and social events. Either that, or I have to find another community to become part of. I do try to maintain social relations with my friends from my 'former' parish."

In a similar vein, **Bob** was once active in his parish but in his seventies was looking elsewhere for spiritual nourishment. "I was a participant in the Church for sixty years. I still take part in a yearly retreat put on by a small group, and I belong to a few small groups made up of people I met when I was active in the Church. But now I get more peace in my heart by not going to church. I don't have to pay attention to what the bishops say or don't say. By and large I find my spirituality elsewhere; it's now more intellectual and scientific. If I were to return, I would need a place I could just walk in and be accepted, where I could stand up with other people who feel the same way I do."

Diane, twenty years younger than Bob, took steps to find a suitable place to worship that fit her needs. By the time she was first interviewed she was a much happier person because of the choices she had made. "I spent so much time focusing on trying to influence power in the Church, and to no avail, that it had a negative impact on my spiritual growth. I began to develop, over twenty years with other like-hearted and spirited souls, an experience of liturgy and community that fed my soul and was in keeping with the teachings of Christ and the Church's history of social justice. When the bishop no longer allowed lay people to share reflections on the Scripture or gay people to receive communion, it was not hard for me to decide to leave the Catholic Church. I realized that I had been letting go of it for years.

"I feel so much more free in the place where we now worship

together. Women are in leadership positions and reflect on the Scripture readings. The community confronts injustices; gays and lesbians are welcomed with open minds and hearts; the liturgies are a shared experience where a priest is not the center of it all. I am happy with this. I no longer have to fight against the institutional Church and its exclusiveness. I continue to pray for the Church, but now from the outside rather than from the inside."

Bridget was a well-educated woman in her forties when first interviewed. She, like Diane, looked at the Church from the outside and had found a home in a community that provided a full scope for her spiritual gifts and aspirations. "The Church that I am serving now sought out and celebrated my gifts. It was an inspired, integrated moment when I realized that as a woman I could serve God and heed my call in an organization that is healthy for me.

"Leaving? This isn't something I did. It was my living experience of God. My decision to leave was because I had to choose between following God's call or following human, *man*-made rules. It wasn't really a choice. The 'aha' moment was *after* I had decided to leave the Catholic Church. I was told I would miss the Eucharist. I don't! Keep in mind, I was taught great Eucharistic theology in Catholic schools, both undergrad and seminary. But there is this *mantra* within the Catholic Church saying 'This is the only way (the Catholic way) that God is truly present.' Not true.

"The Catholic Church brainwashes you; it tells you this is the only game in town. It took me thirty years to see 'the man behind the curtain.' My experience at present is just as valid a means to the Divine. Jesus shows up at other peoples' parties, too! The Protestant Communion, the Protestant community, and the rest of Protestant worship, are just as sustaining. I have had people around me who have been kind and open enough to encourage me to live my truth. I am very fortunate."

Connie, a woman in her fifties, also found a home in a community that welcomed her with open arms. "Ten years ago I joined another church, the Unity Church. A woman friend of mine introduced me to this congregation. Right away I felt at home. They talked of the Mother/Father God; this got to me. Women were equal—God was a woman—women weren't second class, not at all. A woman was the minister leading the church. We also had, for a time, a husband and wife couple as our ministers, and now we have a woman minister again. I can talk to them and they listen."

The Church as a Hindrance

For some, being a Catholic had gotten in the way of their spiritual development. Consider **Nancy**, a woman who was in her sixties in 2011. She had remained a Catholic but more "in name only" in order to support her still-active husband. Because the parish was not providing any spiritual nourishment, she decided to find her own way to pray. "I can't go to church anymore. One of the parish Masses goes on too long, and the earlier liturgy is like a dirge. It's not a pleasant experience for me. I read and pray and meditate a lot. We have a special room in our home that is our 'prayer room.' I pray for all those I read about in the newspaper who have died; I go through the alphabet and pray for all those whose name starts with an a, b, c, and so forth. There is no question in my mind about being saved, with or without going to Mass."

Jamie told a story of growing up in a family of strong faith and spirituality but how she quickly got disillusioned by the actions of a priest and a Catholic school principal. "I grew up in an amazing family environment that formed me and helped me grow in my faith and beliefs. All of us sitting around our family table may not have agreed with each other, but there was an emphasis on the importance of having a faith, however it might be expressed. Going to Catholic schools, on the other hand, didn't always help. I can remember preparing for my first confession. I learned that we confess to a priest because he was a representative of God. I talked to my mother, and we agreed that because we are all God's people, other people can hear our confession as well. They also represented God. So thinking about that, I confessed to my mother. On the day of my first confession, I went into the priest and told him that I didn't have any sins to confess, but I had a message. He responded, 'You have to confess your sins, you can't have a message. But what's your message?' I replied, 'I just want to say thank you to God.' 'You can't just say thank you,' he complained. 'There must be something you've done.' Our voices got louder as we argued so that everyone outside the confessional could hear us. The sister principal asked, 'Is there a problem?' The priest explained what I had said, and I got detention as a result. But instead of causing me shame, my convictions and belief in God grew all the stronger. My mother did have words with the principal afterward, and they came to some agreement so that I was not reprimanded about any of this again. My mother was very supportive in helping us explore our beliefs.

"I was exposed to the broader concept of Church that goes beyond being Catholic. My best friend growing up was Jewish, and we always talked about religion and the difference between being Catholic and being Jewish. Many of my peers were Baptist or belonged to other religions.

"I have explored different churches, both the more rigid ones and the more open ones. Where I now live there are three Lutheran, two Catholic, and a few other churches within a close radius of our home. All the pastors get together, and both my husband and I have been included in those gatherings on occasion. I didn't feel strongly about going to one of the Catholic churches in the area so I went with my husband to his Lutheran community. It was important that we both attended the same church together.

"Being a Christian means helping people around me and helping the larger community. But there doesn't seem to be any connection between liturgy and Christian service. That is when liturgy falls short, as if it were separate from helping people in need. When I was growing up, the larger community was an extension of the liturgy, but now it is not. I grew up with high expectations that there would be a connection. We used to have Mass outside on occasion and then a party afterward. We even had Masses in our home. We all held hands together, it was very intimate and prayerful. Now liturgy is confined to that one room, one worship space. The things that get in the way for me now are not only the presider, the environment, and the music but also the people. I don't have a good connection with the people at liturgy right now."

Chapter 4

Suggestions for Parish Life

Suggested Changes

Toward the end of the first round of interviews every person was asked, "What could a parish do that would help others like yourself feel more at home and engaged?" Those who had moved away from the Church and no longer attended Mass still had many insights to share about the Catholic parish. Their suggestions included:

- Accepting people as they are and listening to their concerns
- Making the liturgies more engaging and relevant to people's lives
- Fostering an inclusive community that is open to all comers
- Dealing openly with social justice issues
- Reaching out to those in need or in trouble

Their responses were also sympathetic and understanding, realizing how difficult change can be for those in positions of parish leadership and authority. **Mark**, a young man who was in his twenties, made this suggestion: "Parishes should have the courage to ask questions without regard to conflicts with the hierarchy. I know of a parish now that is trying to create a welcoming environment for all who wish to join, as well as playing an active part in the surrounding neighborhood. There are still limits to what a pastor and parish can do, but this one is trying its best. Ultimately, if the Church is going to change for the better it will have to happen from the ground up."

Mary Jo was once an active parishioner but had become resigned to her powerlessness to make any changes. She remarked, "The problem is that it all depends on who is the pastor. With fewer men available to be pastors, this limits the supply of good leaders. If married men and women were allowed to be ordained we wouldn't have this problem."

She went on to say, "The level of clericalism among seminarians and new priests is rising. These men are being placed on pedestals, set apart from all others. As a result, they are operating with little or no accountability. Good pastors, on the other hand, are a part of the parish community. They not only are preaching 'Good News'; they are among the people as public figures in the parish and within the surrounding neighborhood community. They not only preach against abortion, they also preach the flip side of supporting and caring for poor young mothers with newborn children." Involved and interactive pastors, in other words, is what Mary Jo felt was needed for a vibrant parish.

Diane, a fifty-five-year-old woman when first interviewed, felt that it was not just up to the pastor to bring life to the parish. "What a parish needs to do is encourage lay leadership so that it is not just the priest who is providing spiritual guidance. Women need to be authentically involved in leadership, including the option to give reflections at Mass. It should not be just the priest who is doing all of the preaching. There should be a variety of others doing this so the community can hear from different perspectives."

Some of those interviewed suggested that the best thing a parish could do was just *listen* to the needs, desires, and insights of the people. **Mark,** quoted earlier in the chapter, had this to say, "I would have to feel that I am welcomed into the parish community. I think this could happen, at least on the local level. Let the laity know that the parish cares about their concerns. When I was in undergraduate studies at a Catholic university

I was involved with a group that decided to stand throughout the Mass. Our purpose was to draw attention to the inequalities in the Church. The ministerial staff responded very well to us. They set up forums after Mass so that people could talk over the issues we were raising. It was hard to hear what some of the folks thought of us, but it was important to have this dialogue. It is crucial for a parish to be engaged in these types of interactive experiences.

"I also feel that most parishes are good at creating opportunities for socializing and community-building events. But there are not many opportunities for people to grapple with issues that bother them, such as concerns with the institutional Church, feeling disjointed or alienated as a Catholic, not feeling 'at home.' A lot of my gay friends don't have a way to talk about being gay and being Catholic. Some parishes have tried to be welcoming to gays, but the bishops have not been receptive to this."

Mike, a forty-year-old "seeker," spoke of his personal experience about how helpful the simple act of listening could be. "What was most helpful to me in my parish was that people listened to me and were not judgmental. That is what a parish could do regarding someone like me. And if someone does come back to church once and awhile, be inclusive, be welcoming, and don't make comments such as, 'Where have you been?' No judging, please, just acceptance. That makes all of the difference.

"Also, make sure that the parish does a good job with outreach ministries to the poor, the homebound, and to inactive Catholics. This reaching out to others in need is very attractive to those who are searching for a parish to join, especially those on the fringes of the parish looking in."

Reaching out to the poor and needy was also suggested by **Arthur**, at one time a highly active parishioner but who no longer attended Mass. His efforts to help others backfired and contributed to his going elsewhere for church, although he did hold out hope for the parish as his remarks revealed. "I joined our parish Social Justice Committee. We would make decisions, and the pastoral council would go along with us. But when the pastor did otherwise, I quit. The pastor would talk to other people in the parish who were not on our committee or on the pastoral council and would go with their advice. As I see it, the pastor got in the way.

"From where I stand, there is no promotion of social justice, no preaching on these subjects, because pastors are afraid of the people who might disagree. The powerful and the mighty who have the money run the show. As a result, social justice on the parish level amounts to a few works of charity but does not affect any systemic change. For the larger Church, as long as you make things dogma and disallow any dialogue and say 'I'm infallible,' no change will happen."

Christina, a woman who was in her forties, agreed with Arthur that the parish could be a place for discussing social justice concerns. "I have visited a Unitarian Church in my area and heard guest speakers talk on current issues. Perhaps a parish could do something like that—bring in people to talk about social issues. It is important not to keep faith separate from people's life choices. There needs to be more integration with the Church and what choices people make, all within a communal context.

"When I was in my teenage years we had a great youth group that was active in our parish. This was important to me because it created a space for teens to discuss issues and make life choices. There was no outside pressure or divisions, and there was huge participation by the youth. What we talked about connected with the teens and their issues. The emphasis was less on preaching and more on applications."

Creating a welcoming, accepting, inclusive environment was mentioned by a number of those interviewed as something important for a parish to work on. This included the young as well as the old, women as much as men, gay as well as straight, those of average means along with the wealthy, both the less and the well educated.

Connie also spoke of feeling included. "When I started at my new church I felt so much at home. There were no judgments made of me by anyone. Catholic parishes should not make judgments, although much of the teachings in the Church are about judging—don't do this, don't do that. In my church of some 350 people there is no judging of one another, even though people come and go. It is such a loving environment. The congregation allowed me to sit in the back when I first joined and cry. People would come up and hug me, but they would not judge. The Catholic parish needs to show people the same compassion and that Jesus is a human being just like ourselves."

Acceptance was also the advice **Rafael** suggested for a parish. From the perspective of a gay person he wrote, "What I think a parish might do is sponsor workshops regarding gay issues. Even to have our local parish welcome and invite gays in would be a good thing. As for sexuality, I feel the parish has a responsibility to understand its younger adults better, stressing the positive aspects of sexuality rather than the negative, and not trying to instill fears so much as the joys."

He went on to say, "I am not sure just how to retain young people as members of the parish. One way would be to make the liturgies more interesting, not just an hour-long service that is the same each week. The liturgical services are so dull and boring. There is so much competition for young people's time these days. The parish needs to understand this and step up to the challenge of providing something that is worth their time and attention."

Bridget, a woman in her forties when first we met, spoke out about what a parish could do. "Let the young women and young gay kids know they can serve God in a healthy organization. That would be a great gift. To parish communities and individual parishioners, I would say. 'Let all the members know that *any* way they choose to serve God is beautiful.' Do not expect the bishops to change this; this must happen on the local level."

Peggy, who had spent a number of years as a religious sister, took a more radical approach. "Perhaps we can do a big 'sit in' to get our voices heard, an 'Occupy Church' sort of thing. The Church needs to give people the freedom to act without being bullied or smashed down.

"The local Church—parish—deals with the everyday lives of the people. It is there to support the spiritual lives of its members. This is done through sacraments and prayer, as well as through social justice and Christian service. Stewardship is a great thing for people to do, that is, what we do with God's gifts. We have to open up the gift and use it."

One way a parish can help people unwrap and share their gifts is through small groups. **Jack,** an older person who no longer considered himself a Catholic, still hung on to a connection with his former parish through a gathering of his friends. "I belong to a small group of people I met at church, and I make a distinction between that group and going to Mass. In the small group there is no 'we have to all believe this or that or we can't stay in the group.' There is a freedom to believe a wide variety of things, and there is no 'if you hold that opinion you can't be here.' There are no requirements to stand up and recite things in unison, no pledges against this or that. None of this is part of our small sharing group."

Andrew joined the Church as a convert. He spoke earlier about a parish being an advocate for social justice. He also wants it to be open and welcoming to all comers. "Openly allow people to get involved. Sometimes longtime volunteers are stuck in their jobs. They need to let go and encourage new involvement. Also, ask people what they want. They no longer come to church out of a sense of obligation; they need to be invited in. Stress the same message for all parishes and small communities—bring people back to Christ. The best pastors can manage large parishes because they don't do it by themselves but encourage everyone to become involved."

Natalie agreed. "The parish community should care for one another, both those within the community and those beyond it.

It needs to reach out to other places that need our help. The people of the parish need to be educated and outgoing to promote this caring for one another."

Colleen went a step further, welcoming everyone no matter their spiritual or political bent. "The Church needs to welcome people for who they are and where they are at in their life journey. It needs to communicate to people that they do not have to fit a mold. If you are there, you are Catholic. If people think a little left or a little right, that's okay. Welcome them in! I would like to remind pastors as they relate to people, 'Be supportive, be understanding, remember that life is hard for many of us and that people need to be nurtured without feeling judged or dismissed.'"

Susie and **Charlie**, a married couple who had moved on, had much the same advice. "The person in the pew just wants leadership to *be real*. It doesn't matter if that person is gay or straight, male or female, married or single. Even younger adults, as conservative as some of them may seem, get this. This is still about faith."

The parish also needs to respond to those in need in very practical and concrete ways. This was the advice from **Jamie**, a woman in her forties when first we spoke who grew up a devout Catholic but then became a member of the Lutheran faith. "At this moment the Church's and the people's needs are running parallel to each other but do not intertwine. I've listened to people who are losing their homes to foreclosure. They are still giving to their church, not money but their time. So when something significant happens in their lives, such as losing a home or a job, I ask them whether they have gone to their church for help. This had never occurred to them. 'Church is where I go to pray, not where I go for help,' they told me. This is such a poor image of Church, so narrow. One family actually did go to their church and asked for help after I encouraged them to do so. Two weeks later I got a phone call. The person was in tears. All she said was, 'Thank you.' The parish community had pulled together a response to the family's need. It wasn't a great deal—a food basket and a small check. But it was something. Now the person feels more able to talk with them and ask for help when it is needed. It doesn't matter what kind of church it may be."

Even though people were no longer active as Catholics, they still had an interest in what the parish had to offer and how it could do a better job. A summary of people's suggestions included the following:

- *Pastors.* Encourage the pastor to be with and among the people, acting in partnership with them and fostering a lay leadership that operates on an equal footing with the pastor.
- *Listening.* Create an attitude in the parish of "We care," not offering solutions so much as hearing and taking to heart the stories people have to tell.
- *Dialogue.* When conflicts or critical issues arise, engage the whole community in a discussion of what might be the best path to follow rather than making unilateral decisions.
- *Welcoming.* Create a culture of inclusion that is open to all, without judgment or discrimination.
- *Liturgies.* Engage the congregation in active communal prayer that stirs in the people an awareness of God's presence and a hunger to keep returning to the worshiping community.
- *Small Groups.* Gather small clusters of people together, making sure there is a safe environment where people can speak freely, where they can agree to disagree while still affirming one another, and are open to growth both individually and as a group.
- *Volunteers.* Allow all parishioners to share their gifts, keeping all areas of involvement open to new people and new ways of doing things.
- *Outreach.* Create a parish-wide reputation of service and acceptance so that anyone who is in need knows that the parish is a place where help and support can be found.

Chapter 5

The Struggles for Those Who Remain

Having heard from those who had decided to move out of the Church and leave the parish, a new group of people now takes center stage. These were the ones who, despite difficulties with the Church or parish, decided to remain Catholics. Of the fifty-five people originally interviewed, thirty-two fit this category. Eleven of them were men and twenty-one, women. All but three were baptized as infants. The ages covered a wide spectrum. Three were in their twenties or early thirties; two were in their late thirties or forties; ten were in their fifties to early sixties; and seventeen were sixty-five years of age or older. The older people chose to remain Catholic in greater numbers than the younger ones.

The topics they chose as the focus for their reflections were similar to those who had left the Church. Seven picked *authority*, three chose *justice*, five centered on *women's issues*, three settled on *sexuality*, three on *liturgy*, two on *young adults*, and the greatest number (nine) reflected on *spirituality*. Chapters 6 through 8 will be centered around these areas of interest. What follows are areas of struggle and frustration among those who chose to remain members of the Catholic Church, even if not as active as they once were.

Church Authority

Issues of authority affected both those who had "moved on" and those who remained. The difference was that the latter group

41

of people had a deep-seated faith that the Spirit was alive in the Catholic Church and believed that this Spirit would not, in the long run, let it fail. There was an energy and "feistiness" that was not found among those quoted in previous chapters. As **Wendy**, a parish staff member mentioned, "More and more of my sense of Church is as the People of God, the Mystical Body, so I don't need to leave it." It is not the people but the institution that caused her problems. "The institutional Church," she continued, "is losing relevance with society, and with myself as well. When I think about authority in my life, I think of my mother and her example. That is what is missing in the Church—not leading by example. It is inauthentic authority."

Ed, ordained a priest but married at the time of the first interview, was hopeful and yet critical of the institution. "I think our Church will grow beyond the present popes who are pushing what they call 'The Reform of the Reform,' that is, as I see it, turning back some of the teachings and reforms of Vatican II. In my mind these reforms are trying to assert hierarchical predominance at the expense of the dignity of the baptized. It is the sin of clericalism. I believe there is a life cycle for the Church that will one day return us to a state of greater inclusivity. The present exclusivity is not in line with Gospel values, especially the egalitarian love that Jesus shows us. For me the present situation in the Church is an 'occasion of sin.' Many people walk out of church angry these days. They are angry at the priest, at the homily, at the Church."

This was a common theme among those who struggled but chose to remain Catholic. **Kathleen**, who at the age of eighty was full of energy and anger whenever the subject of Church or institution was raised. "One reason I remain in the Church is that no 'misbehaving' hierarchy is going to shove me out of *my* Church. At the moment, Church leaders make decisions *for* us, such as what we should or should not read, not giving credit to the rest of the People of God for scholarship, intelligence, and inspiration from the Holy Spirit."

She went on to say, "My anger over this oppressive authority comes from the demands it places on the faithful, especially the poor and less educated in the faith. This oppressive authority is also creating an image of the Church for the world to see. This does not match my view of the Church and the direction it should be heading."

Joanne, a longtime member of a parish staff, explained her feelings toward the institutional Church. "Authority is at the heart of justice issues and flows into so many areas of Church life. It is at the center of a lot of injustice in the Church. Sexism and clericalism flow from the abuse of authority. It pains me what has happened to the sex abuse issue across the world. I think this scandal comes from a misuse of authority. It is heartbreaking to see this happening. That the insular hierarchy trying to protect itself is evil. I don't have much sympathy for the hierarchy because of its inability to collaborate with and appreciate the wisdom of the people it shepherds. It's tragic how much wisdom is out there, and yet the hierarchy fails to utilize the expertise of God's People. It is always too worried about protecting its authority. I can't let myself focus too long on the fact that I continue to practice a religion that so blatantly refuses to honor the gifts of women, which is over half of the Church's population."

Larry, a longtime teacher and at one time an active parishioner, put it this way. "The present swing back to the pre-Vatican Church that is going on today is upsetting. It can't be a good thing. The Jesus Christ I read about in the Scriptures was open and inviting and accepting. This is different from the anger and vengefulness I experience in the Church today. The 'arrogance of authority' continues to keep things hidden and not deal with past mistakes. They do this on purpose. This same arrogant stance goes on in parishes as well, especially in places where the pastor wants to become a bishop eventually."

"The major problem with Church authority these days," recounted **Denise,** an intelligent and thoughtful worker in the Church, "is the growing clericalism. This is a big problem because we had gotten used to priests as our partners. Now the hierarchy is going back to 'Father knows best.'

"The biggest problem for Church authority is that they have educated us as the laity. We were educated in Catholic schools to do research and ask why and then to follow our conscience. That makes it impossible to go back to 'Father knows best,' and not ask any questions. The hierarchy is not speaking for all Catholics, especially women, when they make statements about contraception and a lot of the other gray areas in morality. I don't think Church authorities have thought through these issues, or have considered the individual on whom they are imposing their legislation."

She went on to say, "If the bishops put their money where their 'supposed' mouths are they would be more concerned and more instrumental in finding solutions to the plight of the poor and middle class, treating all people with equality, and caring for the earth's resources. Unfortunately, the Roman Catholic Church is now led by fallible men whose strong self-preservation instinct motivates them to try to control and maintain their power. I distrust just about everything they say and do. The old adage is correct that says 'absolute power corrupts absolutely.' The institutional Church today is a good example of that."

On the other end of the age spectrum, **Anne**, a strong, intelligent women who was in her late sixties, admitted, "The Church's administration is not what I thought it was. I came to ask the question, 'Why should the hierarchy—pope, cardinals, bishops, priests—be held to a different standard than everyone else?'"

These complaints about the hierarchy came from those who chose to remain in the Church. They had, however, a different tone than those who had chosen to move away from the Church. While there was much anger and frustration with various aspects of the institution, this group decided to remain Catholic, at least for the time being. A similar sentiment was uncovered when speaking about justice issues.

Injustices in the Church

The problems that **Caroline**, a women in her fifties, had with the institutional Church were focused more on the local parish and the transitions taking place. She and her husband were forced to leave a parish she loved because of a change in pastors. "I am no longer in my home parish. We have left and joined another smaller Catholic parish in a nearby town. I worry about what will happen when the pastor in our new parish retires.

"When the pastor came into my former parish everything changed for the worse. My husband and I considered leaving the Catholic Church and joining the Lutheran community or some other church. We thought about that for a long time. The reason we didn't leave is that the Catholic Church had so much good to offer, and for me the good outweighs the bad. Some might call me a cafeteria Catholic, picking and choosing what I want, but I'm trying to receive from the Spirit.

"My husband and I have already decided that if the priest in our new parish is changed and is replaced by a pastor similar to the one who took over our old parish that we might have to leave the Catholic Church. We would have to take into consideration many factors before making such a decision.

"There are many good things in the Catholic Church that I would miss—the liturgy, the rituals, the community, the holy days of Christmas and Easter and the like. Being active in a parish like the one we left is like being in a family. The sacraments are awesome, and I value being part of them."

One topic that often surfaced in the first set of interviews was the unjust way women are treated in the Church. **Barbara**, a retired college professor, traced the history of this discrimination: "As both a Catholic and a student of history, I wonder how an institution can ignore its own fundamental doctrine that *all* human beings are made in the image and likeness of God. The overarching example of this 'ignoring' in the Church is the pervasive sin of sexism by Church authorities, illustrated by the exclusion of women from ministries that were present in the early Church, such as that of women deacons. The language and practice of the early Christians pointed to a discipleship of *equals*. This got lost when the Church was 'Romanized' and women were pushed off to the margins.

"Depictions by male theologians and philosophers have demeaned and denigrated women throughout Church history, using language that depicted women as defective males, the gate of the devil, lustful, the source of evil, and the like. This got into the consciousness of the Church all the way to our own time."

Greg, a Catholic school administrator, asked himself, "Have I done enough to understand the current role of women in the world and in the Church? This issue of women is so closely tied to authority. Bishops are not willing to let go of command and control. But at what cost? Women are, by nature, more collegial and collaborative. They could teach the present leadership how to do this."

Among a number of those originally interviewed, patience regarding institutional changes in women's rights was growing thin. **Danielle,** a married women in her fifties, remarked, "Any topic dealing with women's issues is important to me. That's my soapbox. Women's issues include the Church; there is a sin of sexism in the Roman Catholic Church. I'm tired of hearing that the Church moves slowly. I really resent it when a clergy person says, 'Be patient.' How many years must we wait? I would love to be there as the sin of sexism blows open and it is corrected."

Leah, who was a recent college graduate when first we met, had a story to tell about discrimination against women in the Church. "My interest in women's issues began when I started college. A friend asked me my freshman year, 'How do you feel about women not being allowed to be priests?' This question hadn't occurred to me before. My immediate response was, 'I don't feel oppressed at all. Women can be religious sisters, and there are other forms of meaningful involvement open to them in the Catholic Church.' But my friend asked again, 'Do you really believe that, or do you just feel comfortable with that because it's what you grew up with?'

"This conversation was the planting of a seed that has stayed with me ever since. 'What would it be like,' I questioned, 'to have a woman up at the altar sharing the Eucharist with the congregation?' A recent experience of mine raised this issue again. I was attending a school-wide Mass of the Holy Spirit at the start of my senior year at college. I was sitting in the back with my friends, at the end of the pew on the aisle. I was right next to all of the priests as they processed in for the start of Mass. There were about thirty in all. I saw each one of my priest friends that I had learned from and came to respect throughout my years at the Catholic university I attended. I was filled with gratitude and genuine appreciation for the part they had played in my life. It was a few minutes later that I realized these priests were good, good men, but where were the women? This was the first time I felt there might be legitimate movements from the Holy Spirit to change this system in a way that would enable women to share our faith at the altar.

"This realization came out of the blue; I had not expected it as I watched these priest friends of mine. As a result of this experience I wrote a guest editorial to the school newspaper raising the question of women's ordination. What came out of this article were many conversations with my friends. They, like myself, said they had never considered this issue before. At the end of a discussion, regardless of whether we agreed or not, each of them would add, 'Maybe this is a question worth asking.' I also received emails from some of my teachers who were empathetic to what I wrote, thanking me for raising the question, saying this was something that they too struggled with. I was not expecting this, especially from older Catholics, priests included.

"What is scary to me is that dialogue on this issue of women's ordination is not permitted in the Catholic Church at the moment. If the heart of the Church is its people, and change comes from ourselves, that is, from the ground up, I am not sure where this issue will go if it is continually squelched by the hierarchy. There has to be room for dialogue, and there must be a commitment to openness to deal with women's issues in the Church."

Phillip, at the time of our first conversation, had been involved in various parish ministries for much of his adult life. He raised a number of areas where the institutional Church was not acting justly, including its reaction to the gay community. "How can Church authorities," he asked, "consider themselves inclusive when they describe gay people as 'disordered'? How can they consider themselves inclusive if they are the only ones who can put a firm definition on what love is but then deny the right to express that love, especially sacramentally? Who are they to define family? Same-sex couples can provide a loving, healthy home environment just as well as—and sometimes better than—the traditional family. There's absolutely no dialogue! More outrageous and hypocritical is the possibility that many Church leaders are gay themselves but are too afraid to come out of the closet."

Lack of Spirituality

For others, it was not the misuse of authority or injustices that cause them to struggle with the Church, it was something much deeper. The leaders of the Church were not setting people's hearts on fire or giving them something to look forward to, such as a dream, ideal, or call to holiness. **Maureen**, a woman with many years as a pastoral minister and trained spiritual director, experienced this lack among those with whom she attended Mass. "In my experience there are very few Catholic parishes that set people's desires, understanding, or hearts on fire. There is no raising up of the knowledge of God's love and care for us, or the many ways God is in our daily lives and encourages us to be 'Christ for others,' no encouragement to live out our faith in joy. I am saddened as I sit in the sanctuary as a lector and look out at the blank faces of people who seem to be putting in time and performing their duty to attend Mass, coming mostly just out of habit. This is not, in my mind, what a growth in spirituality should be."

Anne, at the time a sixty-five-year-old woman who found Church leadership lacking in truthfulness and accountability, listed two requirements she thought were necessary for authentic spirituality, "I am angered by the hierarchy's refusal to address the sex abuse issue and their refusal and inability to handle it. This includes their inability to admit their failures and to act appropriately in response to the sexual abuse of minors by the clergy. I would like to give them the benefit of the doubt that they are incapable of being honest. But in my heart of hearts I know that their behavior is criminal and that they refuse to do anything about it.

"Many cultures around the world regard inappropriate behavior toward a minor to be subject to criminal prosecution. I fail to understand how cardinals, bishops, and priests could think that their conduct would not be subject to prosecution. Because there is no moral backbone among the hierarchy at the present moment, the result is that we have no authentic leadership in our Church. What is needed is a Vatican III ecumenical council that would include both clergy and laity to discuss just one thing— truthfulness in the Church."

Areas of Struggle before Francis's Election

Some of the issues mentioned by those who chose to remain active Catholics included the following:

- Turning away from the spirit of Vatican II where bishops from around the world pointed the Church in a new direction. "Throw open the windows," was the theme. "Let in the fresh air of God's saving grace by 'reading the signs of the times.'"

The outcome of the bishops' deliberations ushered in an interactive style of worship that was in the language of the people, a sharing in leadership and decision making with those who were not ordained, an appreciation of Scripture as the font and source of revelation, an ecumenical thrust that considered other faiths as legitimate pathways to God. According to some of those interviewed, the windows had been closed and the direction initiated by Vatican II was being thwarted and curtailed.

- Church leaders "making decisions *for* us instead of *with* us," as **Kathleen** described it. She saw this as evidence of a "misbehaving hierarchy." She went on to say, "This behavior is putting a wedge between the bishops and the faithful, especially those 'thinking Catholics' who want to respect the authority of the hierarchy but find that it does not reflect their own values or dictates of their conscience."

- A growing clericalism that is manifested by priests pulling away from being partners with the laity. **Denise** mentioned that it is impossible to go back to a "Father knows best" model of operating, but that is the way some pastors seem to be acting. This was most noticeable when there was a change of pastors, and the new person, as **Caroline** described it, "was neither listening to nor respectful of the people."

- The lack of inclusiveness in welcoming all people to become part of the parish or Church as a whole. This includes those who are gay, minorities, those who don't fit into the mold of a "good Catholic," young people on the fringes, women who feel unappreciated or undervalued for their gifts and aspirations, the divorced and remarried or who use artificial means of birth control.

- Hearts that are not being set on fire. The liturgies, especially the preaching, are not touching hearts and moving people to go out and make a difference. People are not being challenged to "go deeper" in learning about their faith and putting it into action, especially in caring for the poor or those in need.

These were some of the reasons why people struggled with the Church and parish. Despite frustration and anger, they remained active in the Catholic faith. Why was that? It was because of their attitudes toward liturgy, spirituality, and ownership, as the next three chapters will indicate.

Chapter 6

Liturgy and Ritual: The Anchor

What was it that kept these people members of such a flawed and imperfect institution? They admitted having the same struggles as those who had given up on the Church. **Joanne**, a longtime parish staff member, exclaimed, "What do we say? Something like, 'If you find the perfect Church, don't join it because it won't be perfect anymore.' There are truly important things about this Catholic faith that are worth fighting for and sacrificing for."

One of these was the Eucharist as the center and anchor of people's lives. **Maureen**, a liturgical minister, put it this way, "I love good liturgy, and the Vatican II Council encouraged me to come alive when I attended Eucharist. My husband and I were in sync regarding our religious leanings. He volunteered, I volunteered. We had a common dream."

Ed, a priest who chose to leave and get married, tells the story of a faith community that grew in its awareness of the Eucharist as the center of its life and mission. "During the forty-year progression of our community we went from being a parish with a traditional pastor who was fully in charge and making all the decisions to a team experience of leadership. The liturgies became more inclusive, and there was a new sense of self-determination among the parishioners. New social outreach services and programs emerged. All of these social service initiatives flowed out from the parish liturgies and returned back into the liturgies for their strength, giving them life and relevancy.

"The liturgies consistently posed the challenge that being a follower of Jesus makes demands that must be met, that is, that we are to help build a just and loving society. The constant question became: 'What must we do in this neighborhood to bind up the wounds found here?' The Eucharist pumped up people to go out and serve others, and then to come back to Mass for support and fellowship. This approach angered some of the more traditional Catholics, and eventually they left and found a parish that suited their understanding of Church. Others were attracted by this approach and came from a great distance to share our liturgies. They were hungry for this kind of Church and had been searching for a place like our parish.

"Then, a few years ago, a new pastor was assigned to the parish and was given the orders to 'clean up the parish.' What to do? Rather than conform to liturgical rigidity and lose our community, we decided to continue together on our common journey to God. This meant we had to find a place to worship so we could stay together and pray together. We discovered a small Fellowship Hall for Sunday morning Mass. The spirit of our original inclusive faith community is still alive and remains so, no matter what building we end up in.

"Our community is a microcosm of what the larger Church could become. I need to be true to this community that is a gathering of good people who try to live by the Vatican II Council's mandates, not just by the rules. This is very personal to me; I have made a choice, not an easy choice, to stay with the Church as lived out in this context."

Another story was told by **Rachael**, at the time a recent college graduate. "I thought at times about joining a different church, and I have visited other denominations, but I keep coming back to the Eucharist. I can't give that up. I love the Catholic Church, but there are a lot of things I don't really like about it. I'm not sure what my role is in the Church as a young person, what is my place in the wider body of the Catholic Church. Should I work within the structure or outside of it? Should I try to rock the boat and speak out about why we are not responding to the issues of today or go elsewhere? If I choose to step outside of the structure I can be more easily dismissed, but if I stay within I can't be so easily dismissed."

Kristy was a wife and mother who had been active in parish liturgies, especially with the art and environment committee that decorated the church for special occasions. Through this involvement she discovered the link between Eucharist and service. "I am a Vatican II kind of person—open the windows of your mind and let the fresh air in, be inclusive, consider having a married priesthood. I remain in the Church because I love the Eucharist and the opportunity that the liturgy affords me in praying with the people of my community. I also discovered new ways and opportunities for living out the Gospel message. There is so much work to be done helping those who have less or need a helping hand. I wish more of the Church's energy went toward that end."

She described her journey from a thriving parish to a more rigid one when there was a change of pastors. Through it all she remained faithful to the Eucharist and Christian service. "I love our parish. My husband and I helped to rebuild it. We worked with a former pastor who brought it back to life. As a result, our community had an incredible sense of ownership. Everyone felt it. It was *our* parish, not the pastor's. We used our gifts and talents to make the parish better. Pastors come and go, but the parishioners hang in there.

"I myself am not as active now, primarily because I got frustrated with our new pastor. He did not like what we decided in art and environment for the Masses, and I got burned out. I needed more open dialogue and eventually it just became too much of a struggle. There is a liturgical rigidity now. Such a pity."

Lucy, a newcomer to the faith, considered the Eucharist as the core of her faith. "The liturgy is the main place where I have a faith experience; it is the most important thing in my spiritual life. That weekly sanctuary is where I am separated from my daily life, a life that is bombarded with messages that are not always helpful or healthy or honest. When I step into the environment of the Mass it separates me from this secular world. I am forced to spend an hour of my time that is unique from the rest of my life, and this is critical for my spirituality; it is where I want to be.

"The whole experience is one of faith. As a convert to Catholicism I have a sense of belonging when I am at the liturgy. I am a full-fledged member now. It was a choice that came slowly for me. I was missing something, and I would get hints about the need to belong to a church. When I got married to my husband, who grew up Catholic, the opportunity presented itself. Now when I go up for communion I am so grateful to be part of 'the club.'

"I remain a Catholic because the act of attending a weekly service is still a source of spiritual guidance and support. The liturgy provides an hour to meditate, a reminder to mend my ways, to be more forgiving and compassionate, providing a fresh start every week. Usually the message from the homily is sincere and at least partly meaningful and reflective. I love the traditions and the continuity of the rituals.

The Eucharist was also central for **Fayann**. After being active in liturgy for many years, however, her experience changed with the introduction of a new pastor. "I have served on the Liturgy Committee in our parish for the last twenty years. I feel that the liturgy is the action of the Church. It should encourage the inclusion of the assembly in the celebration of the Mass, along with all of the various choices related to how the liturgy is conducted. I enjoyed being active, along with many others, until a year ago.

"The situation changed radically when there was a change of priests to serve our parish community. The new pastor took us back to the pre-Vatican II era almost overnight, with no parish input whatsoever. He claimed that this is what the Vatican II Council wanted, that the priests do everything without any participation of the people. He stressed the adoration of the Blessed Sacrament and brought the tabernacle back from the chapel of repose to right behind the main altar of the sanctuary.

"This change has been cataclysmic for the parish. We are back to the old-fashioned Mass with all of the old rubrics, the whole bit. Although about 10 percent of the parishioners liked the return to the old way of doing things, many others left, and the remaining do not support the priests and their new direction for the parish. Ours was a very participatory assembly. Now we have lost the spark because so many have left the parish. Surrounding parishes who still have a participatory liturgy are picking up new parishioners who used to go here.

"I remain in my parish for two reasons: One is my husband. He has begged me not to leave. He is a cradle Catholic, and I am a convert, having joined the Church while in college at the age of eighteen. I stay because of him. He was educated by the Jesuits and is highly respectful of the Church. The second reason I remain is because if I left I would be deserting the people I love."

For **Jane**, who was over sixty-five years of age when first interviewed, remarked, "As I've gotten older there has been a progression in my spiritual journey. I have begun to feel the presence of the Divine more. This is something that is available to all of us. We can access this through one's religious tradition, whatever that may be. For myself, I do it through my own Catholic tradition. An important piece for me is liturgy; this is helpful to my prayer life. I am comfortable with the Mass at the church I now attend. I find it nourishing. I feel that one is responsible for one's own spiritual development; one needs to be a seeker. It is difficult to be a seeker if you are angry with the Church and expend your energy being critical or negative."

The importance of seeking out what is meaningful was also voiced by **Richard**, a person in his eighties when first interviewed. He had a youthful spirit and a desire for good liturgy. "As a whole, I don't think I am really struggling with the Church. I could not imagine not being part of it, not going to Mass. If

I couldn't find what I needed in our parish—and thankfully it does meet my needs at the moment—then I would shop around and find the right parish that fit my needs, one with a good liturgy and an openness to social justice issues."

The Lure of the Eucharist

These stories about the importance of the liturgy and the celebration of Eucharist revealed one reason people were remaining Catholic. Despite the flaws and shortcomings of the larger Church and the local parish, of the hierarchy or a current pastor, the Mass, with its rituals, Holy Communion, and the gathered community, remained an anchor in people's lives. It was what kept them faithful to their commitment as members of the faithful. The appeal of Christian service and pastoral care flowing out of the Eucharistic celebration also held sway over people's choices to keep returning to the Mass. It provided "spiritual guidance and support," as **Lucy** mentioned, or a place to answer the "call to *be* Eucharist to others," as **Rachael** proclaimed.

The Eucharist was not the whole story about why people remained in the Church, but it was the underpinning that outweighed the imperfection and aberrations experienced throughout the institution, both large scale and small.

Chapter 7

Spirituality as the Source

The Catholic Church has a rich spiritual tradition that is filled with mystics and saints, poets and artists, rituals and devotions, all based on following the teachings and model of Jesus. For many of those interviewed, it was this experience of spirituality, both personal and communal, that kept them Catholic despite struggles and tribulations. Their stories are filled with accounts of this enduring faith against all odds.

Anne, a professional woman in her sixties, was active in parish leadership positions. She considered spirituality as the source and center of her commitment to the Catholic Church. "Spirituality is what keeps one's life together, in both good times and bad. It is the glue that connects us to God. I need the ability to connect with this God as much as possible. The sex abuse crisis has brought me back to spirituality. Before that I was a passive Catholic. Dealing with the sex abuse issue made me rethink what it means to be Catholic. I became an aggressive Catholic, deciding what I needed spiritually rather than letting the priests and Church decide for me. I began to think about my own spirituality and why I should not let the Church do this for me. I only came to this conclusion later in life, knowing that it is never too late to change. I found that I needed to provide the time, space, and effort for my own spiritual life.

"I was not permitted to read the Bible when I was a young girl. I asked my pastor for help, but he slammed the door on me. I have learned that the Church is really about God's Word and about faith. This is what is important to me now. I go to Mass to hear truth from the Gospels. The homilies given at Mass provide my spiritual food for the day."

Fayann, who spoke about Eucharist in the previous chapter, mentioned spirituality as the great "leveler." It involved putting one's gifts to good use. "My feeling is that all souls are embedded with God so that my soul is just as acceptable to God and to Jesus as anyone else's. Jesus didn't have any hierarchy. He selected one person—Peter—to take the responsibility, but Peter was no more influential than was Paul. Paul challenged Peter about making the Gentiles follow Jewish customs. When Jesus gave Peter the keys, all the other apostles and disciples were standing around him. It wasn't only to Peter; each one was given the gifts of miracles, of healing, and of preaching the message of love and salvation. We all have been given this gift to the limits of our abilities and our faith. It is our blessing and our duty to act accordingly."

For Tom, a seventy-four-year-old grandfather when we spoke in 2011, spirituality was centered more on providing a moral compass. This is what kept him active in the Church. "By spirituality I mean the spiritual side of human nature as opposed to the physical and intellectual side. It includes other spiritualities, not necessarily Christian. I myself am centered on Christian spirituality because I was raised Catholic. Spirituality is related to everything that keeps me in the Church. It is the Catholic Church that provides the moral compass to myself, my children, and my grandchildren.

"I'm sticking with the Church because I'm familiar with the opportunities and drawbacks of it. Remaining within the Catholic Church is the only opportunity I see to reinforce the moral compass thing. But it is still a struggle, an intellectual struggle, not a spiritual struggle. My mind goes back and forth but my inner being stays focused."

For others, spirituality was about one's relationship with God and how this affected everything else. Maureen, an older person well versed in spiritual matters, commented, "I am staying with the Catholic Church because of my relationship with God, and because I come from a responsible family. Also because of the call I have received to help people recognize God's action in their lives.

"God is so much a part of my life and this gives me hope. Unfortunately we don't hear about this personal relationship with God from the pulpit these days. The bottom line of all this change and 'shift' is people realizing that their relationship with God has nothing to do with any Church or religion. This relationship with God is the most important thing in our lives. People don't feel the need to leave the Church because being Catholic or Lutheran or Baptist are just words, just institutions. It is what is inside that really counts.

"God does not manipulate or force, but lets free will run its course, always inviting people to conversion and *metanoia*—a change of heart. Jesus did that with the Jewish leaders, and they turned him down so strongly that they had to try to destroy him. God did not will the cross but let it happen and did not get in the way. The same thing is happening today. Poor leaders make poor choices, which in turn cause great harm. God—Jesus— still draws good out of it, as God did out of the cross. There is something much deeper involved here in what the Church is going through just now."

Jane agreed. "As I've gotten older there has been a progression in my spiritual journey. I have begun to feel the presence of the Divine more. This is something that is available to all of us. We can access this through one's religious tradition, whatever that may be. For myself, I do it through my own Catholic tradition.

"Many good Catholic people have influenced my life. A friend told me, 'I'm not going to become something else. I'm a Catholic and I will embrace what I can within it—this tradition is home to me.' There is a lot I don't agree with in the Church, but there is a great richness there as well. It is within the Church where I can find a higher level of spirituality."

Jane's husband, **John,** also found spirituality as an abiding reason for remaining Catholic. "I believe that we are, at our core, spiritual beings. Part of my personal struggle is to continue my search without being separated from the Catholic Church. The Church is too rigid and has tenets that are too strictly bound. In many areas, such as gay rights and gay marriage, the Catholic institution believes it has the 'truth' and is the protector of 'truth.' I can't buy this notion. These truths are still in evolution, and we have not arrived at the end as yet. The Catholic Church would be more acceptable if it admitted that it has changed its own positions in the past, even regarding dogma.

"Given all this, the Catholic Church is still the place I find my roots. This is where I grew up. The Catholic Church is not in the way of my spiritual journey; it is a help. It especially helps me to be part of this faith community. If I leave the Church, where will I go? To a place different but equally imperfect, to some community in which everyone thinks the way I do? Horrors! So I stay, willingly and without apology. It may not be the best Church for everybody, but it works for me."

Ruth was a woman in her fifties when first interviewed. She was employed by a Catholic parish but was not so sure that the Church was the best place for her. It was her understanding of spirituality that kept her Catholic. "Spirituality is where we cultivate our contemplative lives. In contemplation we come to know our oneness with God. But one person is not big enough to hold all the wonder of God. We need relationships, to honor other people's gifts as well as our own. We need to 'be kind, be present, be love' to others.

"I have pondered a great deal how to integrate my spirituality with that of the Roman Catholic Church. I am finding that at this point I am able to integrate the two. I am seeing a much bigger picture in which Catholicism is one means of spiritual expression among many. I do have deep roots in Catholicism, as well as roots that precede Catholicism. I am at this moment working for the Church. I believe there will be a time in the future, perhaps a few years from now, when I will not be depending upon the Church for my livelihood. At that time I may decide not to remain in the Catholic Church.

"A good priest friend had a job opening in his parish, and he invited me to take it. His invitation provided me with an opportunity to use my gifts for the community. I came to realize that I had roots in the Church and that I could tap into its energies. At the present time I am sorting all this out. It's like bread making or pottery—kneading, shaping, being formed. I am not dismissing anything."

As an older person, **Tony** saw it differently. "For most of my seventy-nine years, I identified myself as a Christian, but this Christianity was propped up by the cultural elements of the Church I grew up in. Even my twenty-three years as a priest were mostly spent in feverishly attempting to transform my own spirituality and that of my parishioners. I am remaining Catholic because there is too much unfinished business for me and my faith. Although I would like to see women ordained, married priests, and a less monarchical Church, these things are insignificant in the big picture, which is the mystery of the Father and the Son and the Holy Spirit. After all, the great mystics of history that we acknowledge as saints lived in various Church cultures as different from each other as the age of magical thinking was from today's rational Catholicism, or as the chaotic governance of the early Church was to the iron-fisted curial management that came later.

"This limited and sometimes misleading approach does not adequately represent my God. My God is more mysterious. It is like Zorba's experience in the movie *Zorba the Greek*, 'My God is a Big God.' I don't hear this approach preached very often. This experience of the mystery of God is important to me at this later stage of my life.

"The Church has a collective wisdom and a collective memory of this mystical Christ within and around us. I don't want to leave this memory; it is too important to me. Because of it, I have a foot in the New Heaven and the New Earth, where God is 'all in all.' But I also have a foot in this sinful world of ours. This requires a balancing act. The Church has handed down a revelation that is not subjective, not just my own feelings and experiences. I need this objective balance that comes from the revelation gained through the Church."

Dan, who was not ordained but did attend a seminary as a young man, had a similar way of describing spirituality as Tony did. "I have learned that real spirituality involves 'touching the flesh' and dealing with the corporal realities of the presence of others who surround me in faith, including my family, the wider community, and the good work I have been able to do. These are the things that proclaim that Presence in my life. I have learned that a spirituality that is detached from lived reality and from 'touching the flesh' doesn't work for me. I resisted and rebelled against the sometimes backward formation I received in the seminary. But when we gathered at the 'table of the Lord' something happened that sent us into the world and not away from it. The doctrine of the Mystical Body was not that 'mystical' at all; it was sacramental in the sense of being 'in touch' with the people, with the world, and with the communities to which we as seminarians were sent. We visited apartments and tenements to teach catechism to the children and converse with the parents. This was critical for me as part of my formation. My whole being was being reshaped, both intellectually through my class work and experientially through direct contact with those in need. The frustration for me now is the way the Catholic Church continually manages to let our people down. I myself am complicit in this; it's not just the hierarchy doing it. At the same time, I am fully aware of this Presence in my life that will take me where I need to go. I believe this is a profoundly Catholic stance, and so I remain in the Church."

Finally, **Caroline**, who was a woman in her fifties when first interviewed, described spirituality as "the core of my being—God's Spirit. It is within us all, and I don't take that lightly.

God is our essence and what we are trying to express in our daily lives. People are hungering for an awakening of their Spirit within but they are not aware of this. They are trying in the best way they are able to become complete and whole human beings. They just don't see that it is the Spirit of God that they hunger for. There is a difference between having things in our lives that we can use, and desiring and being possessed by 'things.'

"I was born into the Catholic faith, and I remain open to continuing as a Catholic. For the moment I do this for my own spiritual nourishment. I realize that other faiths and religions could also nourish me as well. The Catholic Church is not the only path to heaven, despite what we hear from the pastor's homilies in our former parish. His sermons were harsh and they limited our Spirit. Every week the homilies were about sin and they brought people down. This is not what I believe about God. This experience has made me grow up as a Christian, not just as a Catholic. I no longer am willing to be led blindly as I was in the past. I am not as accepting of everything any more. This has caused an awakening in me. Now I look at things with my eyes wide open. It has changed me—changed me for the good."

Reasons for Remaining from the Spiritual Side

Those who cited spirituality as the determinate for remaining Catholic mentioned it as being the glue, the great leveler, the moral compass, a mystical union, and the "core of my being." Some themes that emerged included the following:

- Spirituality for these people was a personal decision for God in a Catholic context. The Church provided the tools, traditions, and locus for learning who God was in their lives, especially through Scripture and the Eucharist.
- This personal decision for God implied that no one was better than anyone else in this search. Everyone was offered the gift of spirituality according to one's abilities and faith expe-

riences. It was the personal response of each individual that counted.

- Growing in spirituality included a call to help others. It was a gift that was not to be held to oneself but must be expressed in care and concern for the needs of others.
- One manifestation of spirituality was the Holy Spirit operating as a change agent in the Church. The awareness of this activity gave hope and promise to those struggling with the institution. The Spirit was able to draw out good from bad choices. For example, as **Anne** mentioned, "The sex abuse crisis has brought me back to spirituality."
- The long tradition of mystics experiencing spiritual insights and then sharing these with others provided a rich understanding of Divine Presence in the Church. Although many mystics had to work around the institutional Church at times, they still worked through the Church in pointing the way toward a deeper spirituality.
- Community was an important aspect of spirituality. The Church, gathered in prayer, was a manifestation of what God had instilled in each one of those present. Developing a oneness with God was difficult to do on one's own. There was a collective memory and wisdom of Divine Presence that was not just one's own experience. The Church provided an objective balance.
- Authentic spirituality involved more than a "feeling" of God deep within. It included manifestations of this awareness in one's daily life. As **Dan** said, "Real spirituality involves 'touching the flesh' and dealing with the corporal realities of the presence of others who surround me in faith, including my family, the wider community, and the good work I have been able to do."

Chapter 8

Suggestions for Parish Renewal

Chapter 4 offered ideas from those who had left the Church concerning what a parish might do to maintain a strong vision of a vital, responsive community. Now it is the turn of those who remained members of the Church to offer their insights and suggestions. Those interviewed in 2011–2012 provided a wide spectrum of suggestions, ranging from leadership to liturgy, from formation to outreach, from community building to volunteering. These faithful, struggling, holy people are saying to the local church, "Pay attention to what you are doing and how you function. You are the life-blood of the Church." As **Wendy**, a somewhat disgruntled but still active parish leader observed, "The parish is the only place where the Church is life bringing. There is good energy put into prayer, the Word, sacraments, relationships, and taking care of others. Parishes need a collective voice right now."

The Ring of Authority

For many of those interviewed, what was needed on the parish level was an authority that spoke truth and changed hearts. **Wendy** spoke of pastors when she said, "They need to know they could speak out more about problems with the hierarchy. This is tricky because it can disenfranchise some of the parishioners and could be seen as setting up the parish against the hierarchy. But it is where the energy for change exists."

Leah, who was a young adult fresh out of college, put it more strongly. "As with any organization that deals with life itself, the Church has to be dynamic, not just conforming to a set of rules and regulations. There has to be doubt, struggle, and commitment to growth."

Lay leaders need to exert their authority when things are not going well, at least according to **Danielle,** a woman who was in her fifties when first interviewed. "Women need to be in leadership positions in a parish and be allowed to make decisions that make a difference. Otherwise we will not have a voice that can be heard. We also need to have laity who will speak up and inform the bishop when a pastor is not doing a good job."

For pastors who are trying to do a good job, **Joanne,** herself a parish leader, felt that they could gain authority by exercising a collaborative style of leadership and fostering a vision that was shared by all. "The parish can model shared leadership. A pastor can bear the vision of the people, making decisions in collaboration with the lay leaders. This is not happening at the moment."

She went on to say, "But a parish could be a force and advocate for true collaboration, respecting the gifts and hopes and dreams that the people of the community have to offer. It is important to support the pastor in this shared decision making, calling him to task if need be, and being patient."

Not "lording it over others" was a concern for **Rachael,** a young adult in her early twenties. "The parish needs to offer people opportunities to learn more about their faith, along with insights into other religious traditions, encouraging interfaith and ecumenical dialogue where there are common issues and practices between them and the Catholic Church. It never helps to boast that as Catholics, 'We are the best.' This is a real turnoff for folks."

Authentic authority, the kind that attracts people and brings the parish to life, comes from inner strength. **Ginny,** a religious sister, put it this way, "What I can do at this moment is to keep modeling liturgical leadership that includes women in equal partnership with ordained men. This modeling is one way of counteracting the notion held by so many priests and people that only men can exercise the ministry of ordained priesthood. I will continue to focus on doing what I can do to be a good shepherd to my people, and to do it as well and as effectively as I am able. It is not a question of equal access to ordination; it is a question of whom the Spirit has *called*."

Phillip, who was an adult educator and faithful parishioner, agreed. "It is hard for talented women to listen to less than qualified priests and preachers. It is also hard on women to witness the big church celebrations that are all male-oriented. Get the women up there and include them more. And there needs to be more opportunities like what we are doing in this interview— talking about our feelings toward the Church and parish. I will keep going to church, hoping that my example will make a difference."

Kerry, a person schooled in theology and at one time active in a number of Church organizations, affirmed the need for giving women a greater role. "The Catholic Church is radically impoverished without the leadership of women and their talents. It will become less and less relevant to the women who are not able to exercise their vocation of leadership, which in turn will have an adverse effect on the vocations of their daughters and sons."

She expanded on this greater role of women to include all the baptized, looking to the local parish as where this could happen. "A parish can emphasize and highlight our baptismal rights and responsibilities. The parish needs to cultivate a culture that encourages every baptized person to *be* the Church they want to see happen. We *are* able to affect institutional change and transformation, and have been doing that for two thousand years. I am in favor of anything that rouses us, the laity, out of our lethargy and reminds us of our baptismal agency. I am in favor of identifying the talents and competencies of parishioners and inviting them to use these talents for enriching the faith community."

Ed, at one time an active pastor but now a married person, made this plea: "What a parish can do is hold on to the Gospel over the Church when their demands appear to be in conflict. Put all the energy into loving God and loving your neighbor. Do that and you will live. Keep asking whether the liturgy and parish life reflects the Gospel. As a parish community, does it show itself to be oriented along Gospel lines? If not, then there is a big problem. Follow the marching orders of the Gospel and the rest will take care of itself. Stay with the Gospels and all shall be well."

Liturgy as Life Giving

For those who have chosen to remain Catholic, the celebration of Eucharist is critical. They hunger for homilies that stir their hearts, give them new insights and send them forth to spread the Good News. **Jane** was one such person. "My first place of contact with the parish is the homily at Mass, and this can be a help for my daily life. What I hear must relate the Scriptures to my own life. The homily should help people with their spirituality, and show them how to cope with their problems. The homilist should recognize that people have significant problems and offer people the affirming love of God, the realization that you are not alone. What comes from the mystics is to quiet down and recognize that God is right here. This is the kind of relevance we need from the pulpit.

"Because I am a follower of Jesus; he is present both within and outside me. I experience this presence through the Eucharist—this is my spiritual nourishment. I don't have to accept everything the Church says, but some things are nourishing to me spiritually. I use the Catholic rituals as a help. When people are going through hard times in their lives, they need this help that the Church can provide."

As a young woman who was about to graduate from college, **Allyson** had a good experience of liturgy offered by the Newman

Center near her school. She was apprehensive about what would happen when she left college and moved elsewhere. "After I graduate from college this next year, I hope I can find a parish that is as full of life and possibilities as the one I now attend. This place has solidified my foundation as an active Catholic. Once I leave here and attempt to put my degree into practice in the workplace, I am hoping to find a parish community where I can feel 'at home' and comfortable, learning from the people I meet there as they do from me. I want to stay true to the faith that I have discovered in this parish community, and I will keep searching until I have found it."

Rachael, a young college graduate, described the impact of the Mass in this way: "The Eucharist is something we receive, and we, in turn, give the Eucharist to others. This is a call to *be* Eucharist to others. Mass is fundamentally universal; it unites me to all whom I love, not only living now but all who have gone before and those yet to come. All the more reason to make sure the liturgy is inspiring and touches people's personal lives." She went on to suggest, "A parish should provide a place for people to question their faith and gain insights rather than just going through the motions."

Fostering Community

Given the American cultural drive toward individuality and doing one's own thing, forming a sense of community is a challenge. Some of those interviewed felt this was a critical ingredient of a life-giving parish. **Dan**, who had recently retired from a long career as a pastoral minister, pleaded the case for an inclusive community. "Holiness as understood in our Catholic tradition is a communal reality first and foremost. It is the community that feeds a personal holiness to all who are open to it. It is the community, I believe, that is called to be 'catholic,' that is, be all inclusive. It means bringing in outsiders. The temptation is to protect oneself by not bringing in others who may not agree with us in order to expand the conversation and possibilities. What a parish can do is become a community of faith and outreach, always supporting those who are willing to remain active in the Catholic Church."

Pam, a woman who was in her forties, had strong feelings about fostering inclusive gatherings of young people as a way of building community. "My previous parish had a big block party geared toward younger adults. They would close the streets and have bands and food—like a mini–state fair. Large numbers of young people volunteered to put it on. There were also programs for young adults led by a director on staff who planned socials and fun events.

"That parish also had a strong group of gays and lesbians. Young people would see that this was a good thing the parish was doing. It brought in all the young adults. They didn't want to be part of an organization that was not accepting of all people, no matter their orientation. Young people are so much more open minded about this now, and they want their parish to be the same way. I don't want to see the Catholic Church disappear. We have to keep working at making it more open, making it better."

"Build a community feeling," was the sentiment of **Denise**. "Help people feel welcomed and needed, that they have something worthwhile to contribute. They are not just a face in the pew. Our former pastor, when we asked about forming community, had us come together for dinner and talk about what could happen. This spawned a new group. We didn't need the hierarchy to do any of this; we did it ourselves."

For **Greg**, forming small groups was the secret to a successful parish, some of them operating within the organizational structure and others alongside it as self-starters. "We have fostered small groups that have their own 'liturgies' and rituals. One is a book club at which we discuss important issues through our shared reading. My wife and I also belong to a movie group. Sixteen of us meet in the summer and line up a series of movies to view throughout the year. Our monthly 'movie nights' through-out the year are like a Mass. We gather together and reconnect; we watch the movie together as if we were listening to the Scrip-tures; we break open each one's understanding of the film and its meaning in our lives; and then we share a meal together. That's our Eucharist. I still appreciate the Eucharist that is common to the whole world, but our small movie group is a liturgy as well."

A Commitment to Service

Forming community is critical, but it endures only if it flows out beyond itself into service to and with those in need. **Leah** was a young woman who learned this lesson while spending time abroad. "I spent a semester studying in northwestern India and brought home a strong affirmation of my Catholic roots and her-itage. This has influenced why I now go to Mass, not just to feel comfortable as before, but to be challenged by something beyond an emotional attachment or a sense of comfort, by a spirituality that resides deep within me and persists even through periods of struggle. The shift I had in India was realizing that Catholicism was the religion where I felt 'at home.' Through the Church I can make a commitment to both the piety and service similar to what I found in India. It is something like the sisters who are fol-lowers of Mother [Teresa] who spend long periods in adoration before God and in concrete service to those in need."

Phillip, who attended a multicultural parish, agreed. As he put it, "Parishioners need to rub shoulders with those from other cultures and environments, especially Hispanics. Interchanges with other local parishes that have a different clientele can help a great deal."

Service projects involving a variety of people, especially young adults, was one way of bringing life to a parish accord-ing to **Anne**, a busy professional person who still found time to help others. "What a parish could do is locate young people on the parish rolls, both married and single. Offer them a project that involves direct service to those in need—simple things such as a food pantry or making sandwiches for the daily lunches of school children in need. Get these young adults to work together on a project. This will form them into a group. They could start the project with a little prayer or thought for the day—something from the Gospels. There is no other way to get people back to practicing spirituality and back to the Church. As people do this they recognize the good feelings that come from helping others and how this relates to the Gospels. It is a small movement, but it makes all the difference."

Allyson, herself a young adult, agreed. "First, encourage people to realize their own unique talents and not be afraid to use them in the parish and to help others. It is important that a parish create events where people can share their faith with others and reflect on the gifts they have been given by God. But reflection is not enough. They must find ways to use these gifts in the parish community and beyond. My present parish sponsors mission trips to places away from home. I have spent time in Bolivia, as well as New Orleans, as part of the parish outreach program. This is where students and other parishioners work together, both the young and the old."

Sometimes it only takes one person with a creative idea to change a parish. **Rachael,** a recent college graduate at the time of the first interview, described what happened at her school that blossomed into a significant movement on campus. "Back in the 1980s, a student began something called 'Midnight Runs' after basketball games, reaching out to the homeless on the streets and bringing them sandwiches. Since then, it developed into the largest service organization on campus, with twelve different sites, such as homeless shelters and meal programs served by more than 150 student volunteers.

"The parish could provide projects in which people can easily participate, such as a series that helps people discuss social justice issues and then gets them involved in direct service projects if they wish. We had this on campus, and it helped me explore my faith in ways I never would have had I not attended a Catholic university."

Richard, in his early eighties when first we spoke, held up the parish as the beacon for justice and service. "I see the parish as the primary place to foster social teaching. Our parish has a group that is active in community organizing as a way of responding to concrete needs. The previous pastor was willing to use parish funds to get it started and had a special collection at the Masses to support the effort. It was called *Advocacy Sunday*. The present pastor has continued the support and is behind our efforts. It is now an ecumenical effort involving a number of churches from various denominations. Parishioners are trained to meet with individuals one-on-one to discover each person's concerns and areas of need. It is an exercise in good, active listening. One issue that has surfaced is the need to provide services and support to those with disabilities, especially children. Those with financial resources can afford to pay for special care and education, but the poor do not have that possibility. Our parish's effort to uncover real needs that are going unaddressed has brought forth new leaders for social justice, new advocates for those left unattended."

The Locus of Renewal

Despite the struggles these once-active Catholics have encountered with the Church, they still offered many suggestions about what would make it better, especially on the local level. It starts with confident, creative leadership, including not just the pastor or staff members but lay leaders as well, both women and men. Sharing authority with a large group can get messy, but it opens up people to new initiatives through lively discussion, prayerful discernment, expanded decision making, and mutual problem solving. This is the climate that attracts those with special gifts, abilities, and inclinations to share in parish ministry and leadership. It also opens up the parish to new possibilities and fresh visions. Pastors and staffs can no longer run a parish by themselves. They must reach out and draw in resources from a variety of perspectives and from those of different backgrounds and perspectives.

This sharing of authority can also lead to more attractive and meaningful experiences of worship. People have different impressions and desires for liturgy. Meeting their needs can only be done by providing a variety of Eucharistic celebrations each weekend. The liturgies must be attractive to different parish sub-communities, always seeking to help people pray and grow in their awareness of God's involvement in their lives. As the Second Vatican Council proclaimed, the intent of good liturgy is to foster full and active participation by the congregation. This is the constant challenge facing those leading the service, to keep the Eucharistic celebration alive in people's minds and hearts, and to instill in them a desire to translate the communal prayer experience into serving others.

Building strong and lasting relationships is another aspect of parish life that those interviewed considered an essential ingredient. The key approach is being "inclusive." No one is excluded, no matter their income, age, culture, gender, or orientation. Both large gatherings and small-group encounters are important. Each has its place in helping people interact and break down the barriers of individualism that keep people in their own, self-contained worlds. The regular parish gatherings throughout the year and the spontaneous responses to crises or special one-time events keep the community together and helps everyone, whether long-time parishioners or recent arrivals, realize that there is something special here that is greater than what any group or individual could create on their own. The Spirit is alive in the midst of the assembled gathering, whether large or small. A successful parish knows how to keep tapping into that Spirit-power, that energy that holds the parish together and keeps it moving forward.

Being a Catholic parish, however, is much more than a community coming together to celebrate Eucharist and enjoying one another's company. It must be "on a mission." Every member must come to know that "we are not here for ourselves; we are here *for others*." Service is the proof that the parish is living up to its calling as an extension of Christ in the world. Those who remain in the Church and local parish realize this, as the first set of interviews revealed. **Richard** mentioned that an authentic parish must "uncover real needs that are going unaddressed" and bring forth "leaders for social justice, new advocates for those left unattended." It is the parish that provides the outlets, the organizational structure, the training and orientation not usually available to individuals. As **Phillip** mentioned, "We need to do this simply because God said so. We are here to help our fellow human beings. Let's do it as a group." That's called *parish*.

These are some of the avenues for parish renewal coming from those who chose to remain "Catholic in the midst of turmoil." But unknown to any of those originally interviewed, change was in the wings. The Holy Spirit breathed on the earth and presented a gift of great value to us all.

Reactions to Pope Francis

I myself will search for my sheep,
and will seek them out.
As a shepherd seeks out his flock
when he is among his scattered sheep,
so I will seek out my sheep. . . .
I will bring back the strayed,
and I will bind up the injured,
and I will strengthen the weak,
but the fat and the strong I will destroy.
I will feed my sheep with justice.
                                       Ezekiel 34:11–12, 15–16

What's Changed and What Hasn't

On March 13, 2013, Francis was elected as the new pope of the Catholic Church. Much changed at that moment. It was clear that however people felt about the Church before that date, they would be feeling differently from that moment on. The interviews recounted in the first part of this book were people's opinions recorded in 2011–2012. But to what extent would their attitudes change because of Francis becoming pope? Once the shock, and in some cases, the euphoria of his early actions, comments, and priorities had died down, to what extent would those interviewed earlier be influenced by his way of proceeding? It would take some time for his presence as pope to sink in and make a difference. That is the reason for the four-year interval between his election and the commencement of a second round of interviews. No longer would the question be, "Why have you, who were once active in the Church and parish, pulled back from your involvement or even left it completely?" Now the question is, "Has Pope Francis made a difference in your view of the Catholic Church, and to what extent has his papacy changed your attitudes or level of involvement?" Before considering the responses from those originally interviewed, the next chapter will attend to the opinions of Pope Francis from a wider perspective.

Chapter 9

The Current State of Affairs

As mentioned in Chapter 1, the Pew Religious Landscape Survey of Catholics in 2007 reported that 32 percent of Catholics baptized as infants no longer called themselves Catholic. By 2015, the Pew Research Center realized that measuring those who were Catholic and those who were not was a more complex issue. This resulted in a new survey that included a wider range of identities and connections to the Catholic Church than previous polls had uncovered.

The results from the second survey found that the percentage of adult Catholics in the United States had dropped from 24 percent in 2007 to 21 percent in 2015. However, it found that as many as 45 percent of Americans had some personal connection to Catholicism (Pew Research Center Survey of U.S. Catholics and Family Life, May/June 2015). The new survey report divided this figure of 45 percent into four categories:

• *Catholics.* These are the people who, when asked, "What is your present religion, if any?" say they are Catholic. This is the 21 percent of the country's adult population mentioned above. Of this number, 39 percent attend Mass at least once a week; another 45 percent come once or twice a month or less often, leaving 16 percent who come rarely but still consider themselves Catholic. These people are loyal to the Catholic Church, and most (70%) say they could never imagine leaving Catholicism.

- **Ex-Catholics.** Beyond the 21 percent who call themselves Catholics is another 9 percent who were raised in the Catholic Church but no longer consider themselves Catholic in any way. But not all ex-Catholics appear to be completely alienated from the Church. A majority (59%) give Pope Francis positive ratings, and a few (10%) say they go to Mass occasionally, at least once or twice a year; and 9 percent would choose to receive the sacrament of the sick if they were seriously ill.
- **Cultural Catholics.** This group amounts to another 9 percent of Americans who consider themselves to be Catholic in some way, although they may belong to another faith, most often Protestantism, or are religiously unaffiliated. When asked to explain why they considered themselves Catholic, most of them mentioned being raised in the faith, which meant that they still thought of themselves as indelibly Catholic by culture, ancestry, ethnicity, or family tradition. A smaller number said they were not raised in the Catholic Church but had some other attachment, such as being married to a Catholic or having a Catholic partner and therefore thought of themselves as partially Catholic even though Catholicism was not their own faith. Cultural Catholics generally express an affinity for the Church and have a high positive approval rating of Pope Francis (73%).
- **Other Connections.** About 8 percent of Americans were not raised Catholic and do not consider themselves Catholic, but nevertheless say they have some familial or institutional connection to the Catholic Church. This group includes people who had a Catholic parent but were not brought up in the faith. It also includes some non-Catholics who say they attend Mass at a Catholic parish at least a few times a year, as well as those who have a Catholic spouse or partner but who say they don't think of themselves personally as Catholic in any way."

The Pew Research Center Survey of U.S. Catholics and Family Life made this observation: "Since Pope Francis' election in 2013, there has been much discussion of a potential 'Francis effect,' with some commentators speculating that the popular pope, and the winds of change he has brought to the Church, might draw more former Catholics back to the fold. The survey suggests that the most likely candidates to be drawn back by a Francis effect are in the Cultural Catholic category" (Pew Research Center Survey Report, September 2, 2015).

A few comments from those interviewed who had left the Church but could be considered "Cultural Catholics" are revealing. **Theresa,** who left the Church when she was a teenager, mentioned, "It will be easier for me to be a member of the Catholic Church now and to attend Mass. I no longer [because of Pope Francis] have to stay away because it goes against my principles. I don't have to stay away from 'that Church' because of all the things that I don't stand for. I would not mind being affiliated with the Church and being called Catholic now. That is true and it's okay."

Mark, a young man in his late twenties, put it this way, "If I could find a place that is more open and includes women and gays on an equal basis, I would be willing to try it out, I mean, return to the Catholic Church."

Fanny, a thirty-year-old Hispanic, defines her ties to the Church this way: "My spiritual life is very complicated—I am a cultural hybrid. I am Latina; I am Mexican; I have been in American for half my life. A lot of my own beliefs about religion conflict with my family's belief."

Changes in Attitudes

The Pew Research Center Survey Report (September 2, 2015) asked whether Catholics believed the Church should change its position on a variety of issues. One of these was artificial means of birth control. Three-fourths of those who identified themselves as Catholic (76%) expressed a desire to have the Church allow the use of birth control. Eighty-one percent of the ex-Catholics (81%) felt the same way, as did 84 percent of the cultural Catholics.

Attitudes toward homosexuality and gay marriage have shifted significantly in recent years. Between 2007 and 2014, the percentage of Catholics who thought that homosexuality should be accepted went from 58 percent to 70 percent in just seven years. Among self-identified Catholics in 2013, the year the pope was elected, 54 percent of them supported same-sex marriage. By 2017, the figure had risen to 68 percent, an increase of 14 percent. The ex-Catholics and cultural Catholics had an even higher level of support for gay marriage.

Regarding regulations concerning priestly ordination, the Pew Research Center Survey (September 2, 2015) found that 62 percent of the Catholics felt that the Church should allow priests to marry, compared with 79 percent of the ex-Catholics and 83 percent of the cultural Catholics. A similar trend was found regarding women being ordained to the priesthood. Almost three out of five Catholics (59%) thought this should happen, as did 66 percent of the ex-Catholics and 77 percent of the cultural Catholics.

These shifts in attitudes are the result of many relevant factors and influences coming from both within and outside the Catholic Church. It is difficult to measure just how much of this is due to Francis becoming pope. On the other hand, in a survey report published by the Pew Research Center on March 6, 2014, just one year after Francis's pontificate began, 71 percent of U.S. Catholics said that he represented a major change in direction for the Church. Two-thirds (68%) felt it was a change for the better. Three years later, a Pew Research Center Report dated January 18, 2017, remarked, "Pope Francis is more popular among U.S. Catholics than he is among the public as a whole, with eight in ten or more American Catholics routinely giving the pope favorable ratings. Currently, 87 percent of Catholics express a favorable view of the Pope."

These statistics provide a cross-section of attitudes and opinions but not the personal feelings of individuals, both those remaining in the Church and those who have chosen to leave.

Has the election of Pope Francis made a difference to these people, and if so, in what ways?

Before seeking to answer that question, one other aspect of the current state of affairs in the Catholic Church needs to be mentioned. It is the negative reaction toward Pope Francis that is coming from some of the more conservative members of the hierarchy and a small minority of the laity. An online article in *The Guardian*, entitled "The War Against Pope Francis," touched upon some of the issues that have caused difficulty for these people (theguardian.com/news/2017/oct/27/the-war-against-pope-francis).

"Outside the Church," the article mentioned, "Pope Francis is hugely popular as a figure of almost ostentatious modesty and humility. From the moment that Cardinal Bergoglio became pope in 2013, his gestures caught the world's imagination: the new pope drove a Fiat, carried his own bags and settled his own bills in hotels; he asked, of gay people, 'Who am I to judge?' and washed the feet of Muslim women refugees.

"But within the Church, Francis has provoked a ferocious backlash from conservatives who fear that this spirit will divide the Church, and could even shatter it. . . . From his swift renunciation of the pomp of the Vatican, which served notice to the Church's 3,000-strong civil servants in the Roman Curia that he meant to be in charge, to his support of migrants, his attacks on global capitalism and, most of all, his moves to re-examine the Church's teachings about sex, he has scandalized reactionaries and conservatives" (p. 1). **Kristy,** an older person who has remained a Catholic, mentioned, "The problem is that the conservative archbishops and bishops are still working on the old policies. I don't think they like him. The old guard is not moving out."

The conflicts between those who reacted against Pope Francis came to a head in a document he wrote following the bishops Synod on the Family in 2015–2016. The document is called *The Joy of Love (Amoris Laetitia)*. "The dynamite," the *Guardian* article continued, "is buried in footnote 351 of Chapter Eight, and has taken on immense importance in the subsequent convulsions. The footnote appends a passage worth quoting, both for what it says and how it says it. What it says is clear: some people living in second marriages (or civil partnerships) can be living in God's grace, can love and can also grow in the life of grace and charity, while receiving the Church's help to this end. Even the footnote, which says that such couples may receive communion if they have confessed their sins, approaches the matter with circumspection: 'In certain cases, this can include the help of the sacraments. I want to remind priests that the confessional must not be a torture chamber, but rather an encounter with the Lord's mercy. I would also point out that the Eucharist is not a prize for the perfect, but a powerful medicine and nourishment for the weak. By thinking that everything is black and white, we sometimes close off the way of grace and growth'" (pp. 10–11).

The article went on to affirm that *Amoris Laetitia* "is an example of the Church learning from experience. But that is hard for conservatives to assimilate: historically, these bursts of learning have only happened in convulsions, centuries apart. This one has come only 60 years after the last burst following Vatican II, and only 16 years after John Paul II reiterated the old, hard line" (p. 11).

The chapters that follow report on the feelings and aspirations of both those who have left the Catholic Church and those who have remained, although they may not be as active as they once were. These are not hard-line or conservative people who dislike Pope Francis and the direction he is heading. Quite the opposite. They love Francis, even those who are no longer members of the Catholic faith. In fact, many of them want more rather than less change. As **Kristy** put it, "Things are not moving fast enough for me. I want a more liberal Church, a more inclusive Church, a Church that is welcoming to everybody." The stories begin with those who at one time were active and loyal Catholics but are now at a distance from the Church they once called home.

Chapter 10

From Those Who Have Left

The Pope's Image

"I love the pope," remarked **Bob**. "He is the best thing that has happened to the institutional Church in the last forty to fifty years. Francis is a breath of fresh air." Many others who, like Bob, no longer consider themselves Catholics had similar impressions of Pope Francis.

Some of the aspects of his image include: being humble, simple in lifestyle, a good listener, happy to be with people, approachable and unassuming. **Jamie**, a cultural Catholic because of her strong ties with her family of origin, stated, "He could come over to my house, and both he and my family would feel comfortable. My impression is that he would be very welcome around the dining room table. He would come in as a friend of my brother and sit in my dad's chair. He seems approachable, easy to talk to, he would listen well."

Diane's image of Francis was that of a very spiritual person with a strong interior life. "He is a principled man who applies his spirituality to his values. He is a really evolving, integrated person. He applies his beliefs in Christ to today's world."

A number of these former Catholics were attracted to Francis because he exuded an image of being "one with" others and approaching them as an equal. **Mark**, another cultural Catholic, expressed it this way, "When he first was elected, he came to eat in the Vatican cafeteria and was interacting with the workers. That meant a lot to Catholic workers in the United States, to see their leader recognizing others as equal. I think that is genuine; this is what he does. He is not someone you would think of being the leader of one of the largest corporations on the planet. This is a good image for the Church."

Others found Francis not only someone who listened and was attentive to others, he was also a voice for social justice that could take the Church in a new direction. **Colleen** described him this way: "He seems to feel he is a servant to people rather than an overarching leader. I was happy that he was very humble and had some different views, and I thought that he was pretty progressive for the Church."

"I am very positive toward Francis," remarked **Peggy**, at one time a very active Catholic but who now is at some distance from the Church. She praised his focus on Christ as a "freeing aspect of his papacy. This is a Jesus-oriented pope. The communication of his image happened quickly."

Rafael, a young Hispanic nonbeliever, appreciated the pope's breadth of knowledge and interest, covering both the scientific and the personal sides. "He seems to me more science oriented. I am happy to see a pope who embraces science and tries to communicate this to people. Religious people who are not Catholic see his humility, and it changes their outlook. They don't see this pope as just a rich man sitting on a golden throne. He has made a point by saying through his actions, 'This is not the way I am going to live my papacy.' There was a shift with Francis when he first came out on the papal balcony with just a plain white gown. He is challenging us to live simpler and take care of each other. This is his vision—like he is a Jesus figure. He is putting out a message of embracing people, not just tolerating them."

Sally was also challenged by Pope Francis. "Yes, he has made a difference in my attitudes and my thoughts." She was pleased to see that he made an impression on her adult daughter as well: "I have a daughter who has left the Church, and not just the

Church, but God and everything. The pope has actually caught her attention. She isn't ready to go back yet, but it made me happy to hear that she saw him as loving and open. I also like his image of openness because I experienced a very closed reception in the past."

One image of the pope that these former Catholics described was that he had a universal appeal that was not directed just to those within the Church. **Theresa** stated, "He has a good reputation with almost everybody. This makes him powerful because if he says something, everyone will believe it. They know that it came from the right place and will not be self-serving. They also know that he speaks for all people and not just for Catholics; there is no nationalism or parochialism about him. He is completely different from the few popes who came before him. He sees people just as Jesus did. He walks the streets as if he were in Canaan and that everyone who meets him feels it is like meeting Jesus. I think that is what Francis does."

Connie is more of a cultural Catholic because she is searching for a church where she can feel at home and be part of a community. Not finding that in her local Catholic parish, she thought she had found it in a nondenominational Unity Church. Soon, however, she became disillusioned because of the infighting and lack of harmony there. She is still searching, but the pope has given her new hope. "I am really excited that he is the pope because he is so open minded and humble. I wish I were more humble, that I could walk in someone else's shoes, could focus on the positive side, could question things and find the gray area, could give people a chance because every situation is different, could break down the old traditions that say, 'We have always done it this way.'"

A Change of Emphasis

Most of those who have distanced themselves from the Catholic Church are delighted with the fresh direction Pope Francis is taking. His focus is more on the poor, the forgotten, the disen-franchised, and those on the margins. **Mary Jo**, who is some-where between an ex-Catholic and a cultural Catholic, put it this way: "He clearly identifies with the people who are not part of the mainstream, of the power structure and the wealthy of the world. His message resonates with Jesus's message."

Mike, now an Episcopalian, was very surprised when Francis was elected pope. It gave him a new sense of hope, although, in his words, "It was too late for me to come back to the Catholic Church." He went on to say, "I like his image of the Church as a 'field hospital'—I really like that image—that is what we are supposed to be doing."

Besides siding with the poor and marginalized, Francis has also changed the emphasis away from stressing rules and regulations to focusing on the unique situation of each individual person. He is concentrating on needs more than on requirements. **Mark**, a young man who is considering returning to a Catholic par-ish, made a comparison between Pope Benedict XVI's approach and Pope Francis's emphasis. "Unlike Benedict who was more hierarchical and would say, 'These are the rules, this is the way it is,' Francis feels much more like, 'We are the Church.' He is a pastoral pope, while Benedict had a top-down way of being pope." Mark has concerns about which of these two approaches will win out and how it will affect his own faith journey. "Every time I inch ahead to become involved," he mentioned, "I get this idea that more of the progressive laity have left the Church and the conservatives have stuck around. These are the folks, I fear, who are going to take over the Church. The pope's challenge is how to make the Church relevant in this world today."

Nancy had much difficulty with the Church until Francis became pope. She remarked, "If Jesus lives in every heart, there should be no one excluded. There should not be the rigidity of words and rules. I would like to see him dissolve all the rules into a much simpler message of being kind, sharing with one another, and being humble."

Jonathan, a young, gay ex-Catholic agreed. "I liked that he spoke on what I think are the important things and what Jesus Christ would have wanted the Church to focus on. These include poverty, equality, climate change—that is a good direction for the Church to be moving in, instead of getting bogged down in some of the other moral issues that the Church has been involved in."

This struck a chord with a number of others who have distanced themselves from the Church. Peggy, a former religious sister who stopped attending church, mentioned, "This is a Jesus-oriented pope instead of a religious-oriented pope who stresses rules and regulations." Rafael added, "I think the Church has to clean house. Stop going back and forth about who can receive communion or reconciliation or confirmation. How can Jesus care about all of this?" A similar sentiment came from Connie: "He is opening up the doors to so many things. He is not emphasizing the laws or rules. Francis is bringing the Church home to us, which is where it should be in the first place. That's wholesome to me, that there can be changes in the Church. Even if he doesn't change the laws in the Church, his perception is different. That will encourage people to see things from a different angle, and it will create dialogue and change."

Sally, a woman in her fifties, had moved out of the Church because, in her words, "the stifling rules seemed to bring down my children rather than encourage their spiritual growth." Now, looking in from the outside, she found some of the requirements amusing. "The rules and regulations kind of crack me up. When we were at dinner with friends, the hostess said, 'Oh, we are allowed to eat meat on St. Patrick's Day (a Friday during Lent).' Who makes up these rules?" Sally exclaimed. She went on to admit, "But Francis is more open. Now people are listening—they are following his tweets—it's good that they are getting his messages."

Theresa, someone who would be willing to try out the Catholic Church once again if she could find a parish that fit her needs and inclinations, liked the priorities of Francis. "What I hope will happen with this pope is that the younger people will focus more on love than on laws. I hope the older people are willing to accept others even if they are not in the Church, no matter who they are, whether they are Jewish or anything else. They are part of the human church, part of the new covenant, instead of being driven by laws. He can't do everything, of course. I don't struggle with this because I grew up in a culture where some of the 'laws' were restrictive, but we didn't have to adhere to them too strictly; we grew up in freedom. My friends struggle with this and go running and screaming to other churches, such as the Unitarians or no church at all. I also see a lot of young folks carrying the flag against abortion and want all of us to follow 'the rules.' Of course, none of us like abortion, but to judge others is wrong—they should not be the judges. Again, let's focus on the love thing and not on the law thing." **Fanny**, a young Hispanic woman, agreed. "People have to practice birth control because they are poor and can't afford more pregnancies—the pope should not condemn them."

Francis and the Institution

One area where people felt Francis was making a difference was his outspoken criticism of clericalism and the exercise of hierarchical privilege among those in positions of authority. On more than one occasion he challenged members of the Roman Curia to act as servants and stewards rather than exercising power over others. **Mary Jo** was pleased he was doing this, "I like that he has torn down the wall of clericalism a little bit."

This action by Francis of confronting and calling into question various aspects of the Church's institution led to the inclusion of this question in the second round of interviews: "Is Pope Francis the same as or different from the institution that is made up of those in positions of authority in the Church, whether cardinals or members of the Roman Curia, bishops or pastors of a local parish?" The responses were revealing. Some had difficulty responding because they were no longer practicing Catholics and as a result had little knowledge of the institution. Others, while not active, had much to offer.

Those who felt Pope Francis was part of the institution included **Diane,** who said, "I think he is definitely part of the institution and was selected to be part of it. People were leaving the Church because it was not relevant; that is why he was elected. Those who elected him saw this, and they trusted his moral balance. They took a risk, and that was remarkable because many people are reactionary." She also saw the pope as the Martin Luther of our times. "He has looked at all of the traditions and self-perpetuating positions and buildings that were basically supporting those who were there and who had the power but with limited response to people in need. Instead of dealing with the sexual abuse issue, for instance, they were protected within their own environment. Francis is breaking up the temple, as Christ did, making the Church more relevant and vibrant. The institution needs to be in place, and there is beauty around the institution that should be protected. I think Francis is in the institution insofar as he is able to do what he is doing. He has been very clear about responding in love to everything we do. He is somebody who is not defensive or trying to protect and keep the institution the same as it always has been. I find Francis a wonderful spiritual leader and he inspires me, but the institutional Church is part of the problem."

Trish felt he is part of the institution but knows how difficult his job is. "He is working his way through the stonewalling in the Curia. The hierarchy is changing in the ways they deal with each other, in not doing things always the way it used to be done." **Peggy** felt the same way. "The pope has to walk a fine line—some people love him and some people hate him. Just as the bishops have trouble with this pope, they would have had trouble with Jesus as well." She went on to say, "Francis is ticking off the bishops and priests, that is, the hierarchy, because his values are the values of Jesus. He is saying, 'Remember who Jesus was on earth, what he himself said and did. Jesus said, 'Don't judge, heal where you can heal, feed where you can feed. Love people.' Francis is ready for this."

Rafael used almost an identical image of walking a fine line. "I think he is limited by the dogma of the Church. If he didn't have the checks and balances from the top, he would be more proactive than he already is. I think he is tiptoeing a fine line between being an activist but not being an activist. That is what a leader should do. Francis drives the Church. In such a large institution, that is really hard to do."

Others felt the pope was not a part of the institution. This included Mary Jo, who explained, "He is an individual and so no, he is not the same as the Church institution. But he carries the culture of the Church. He is the pillar, the icon of the Church, the center of the Church, and as such, the buck stops there. I cut him some slack because I think it is difficult to come into any institution that has gone so far from the center, by that I mean, Jesus Christ and the Gospel message. It is difficult to come into that and make changes in order to bring people back to that center—it takes time, it takes patience, it takes the right people around you, and it takes an open heart and mind. I hope Francis can live long enough to swing that pendulum a little further, but it is a big job."

Andrew is more graphic in his description of Francis working against the institution. "He is trying to remain independent from the institution, but he is being affected by it. It is a giant, megaglobal corporation. Inclusivity is the one area I see he is trying to make happen. That autocratic, legalistic style of leadership is not being followed in any type of group these days, no matter the institution or the organization. Francis is pulling the hierarchy, kicking and screaming, in this direction. It is a big challenge, but this is what it would take."

Susie and Charlie, a married couple who joined the Unitarian-Universalist Church, agreed. "Francis is more separate from the institution, not entirely part of it. He must be true to himself and step aside from his role as pope if it gets in the way." Susie went on to add, "I sympathize with him because it must be really tough to work around the system or within the system. I do appreciate that he is so vocal about many things, and as a result, many in the Church leadership are not happy with what he says. But he is still going to say it the way it is."

One way the pope is not part of the institution is that he is not in favor of all the trappings and frills associated with the hierarchy. As **Nancy** mentioned, "The pope comes off as being very genuine, but all of the trappings makes that difficult." **Jamie** said the same thing. "The bishops come into the parish, and they have the whole garb and everything. What I am most struck by with Francis is that he is saying no to all this. I am proud that he is the pope and doing this. It made me think, 'Wow, this is a big change in the perception of the hierarchy. This is good!' He has a lot of those who are sandwiched between what the people want and the local congregation wants, and what he is about. The hierarchy in the middle isn't delivering his message. Jesus just got out there and did all the things he did. He did not need a lot of people to deliver his message. Sometimes people get in the way. The pope needs to have a powwow with all of the Church leaders and tell them what he wants."

The institution had a big impact on **Mike**, a man now in his forties who was once a member of a religious order but left not only the order but the Catholic Church as well. "The institutional Church is what pushed me out. The change in pope has not filtered down to the local level. The institution is still present. I hope Francis will live long enough to appoint more good bishops. The way I see it, the people respect the pope but not the institution. The doors of the Church need to open out—and it's not just because of a fire code. Local Church depends on the local bishop more than on the pope. It seems as though the pope is separate from the rest of the Church—he deserves a lot of respect, but the rest of the Church hierarchy does not. Francis has raised expectations of what is possible but this has not happened—high expectations go unrealized."

Theresa was more hopeful. The way she put it, "He is a surprise to the hierarchy. He is not the same as the hierarchy—he is not driven by fear. I think most of the time we bring people into power out of fear that we won't have someone like ourselves—it's a matter of power. I think Francis sees people as equals."

Not Returning or "Perhaps"

Pope Francis has had an affect on all twenty-one persons who were at one time active members but have chosen to stop practicing their Catholic faith. Even though they may no longer attend Mass or participate in the life of a parish, they still feel the influence of Francis in their lives, in their attitudes, and in their aspirations. The question is, to what extent did his election as pope draw them back closer to the Church. All twenty-one gave an answer to this question.

Fifteen of them said they had made up their mind and, although they liked his leadership style and priorities, his values and interaction with ordinary people, they have decided to continue along the same path they had chosen before his election. For the remaining six, their comments suggested an openness to returning to active involvement in the Church and parish, but only if they could find a place that matched their religious desires and spiritual inclinations. Because of Pope Francis, **Christina** affirmed, "I am now proud of my connection to the Catholic Church. I no longer can give up on the Church."

This division between those who have made a definite choice to remain outside the Catholic faith and those who show an openness to perhaps returning to the Church reflects the distinction between ex-Catholics and cultural Catholics. There are many nuances that blur the boundaries between these two groups, but their own comments revealed that such a division does exist.

With regard to those who have left the Church and would not return, **Mary Jo** had one of the strongest responses. There was no doubt in her mind where she stood. "Pope Francis hasn't made any difference to me. I was gone before he was elected, and am very comfortably gone. I was done grieving my past with the Church, and Francis becoming pope did not cause me to revisit that decision. I was heartened and excited about his election because of the opportunity for change in the Catholic Church, but that did not cause me to rethink the decision I had previously made. Pope Francis doesn't influence my attitudes or behaviors in any way."

Andrew was also convinced that the spiritual home he had discovered fit him well, especially because of the experience of community he found there, something that was lacking in his Catholic parish. "I am now involved in a nondenominational Church—the Community Christian Church. I won't be going back to the Catholic Church; the appeal is gone for me. The place we go to now is much more dynamic. My church now is so much more energetic and is more like a community. The Catholic Church feels to me more ritualistic instead of focusing on the community. If you go back to the early Church, the people met wherever they could, on a mountain or a hill or in a house—it was much more of a community without buildings. The church where we go now is much like that. It's more focused on bringing people back to God. This is the mission of our church—helping people find their way back to God."

A married couple who had joined another religion decided to stay put. **Susie** exclaimed, "As time goes on, I give Francis a thumbs up for what he is doing—he is doing great stuff. But we had already made our decision to leave the Catholic Church before he was elected. Some of the Unitarians have asked us what we think about Francis. We think very highly of him, but it wouldn't have made us stay in Catholicism, nor is it bringing us back to the Catholic Church. By the time Francis was elected, it was too late for us. We had moved on to another religious affiliation."

For **Jack**, there is a sense of loss from leaving the Church, a pull he experiences because of the people he met in his previous parish and the formation of a strong community he still cherishes. His own words speak of this longing, "Francis's election was a good thing. I am not, however, changing my attitude toward the Church. At the moment I am standing outside the Church institution, but I am still in relation to other people as part of my community." There was a sense of loss for **Mike** as well: "I have peace that I'll not be a Catholic again. There is a tinge of sadness of what I have left behind, but I have no skin in the game anymore. I wish the pope well, but it's not my Church now. Life moves on. I am not angry anymore, but hope for the best. Once you are Catholic, however, it is still in your bones. At the same time, I am where I am supposed to be right now. It is not my Church, nor, at this point, could it be. When our first interview took place, I had left my religious order just a year before, so my experience of this and of the Catholic Church was all still raw."

Diane has found a new community that satisfies her needs, although Francis still has a strong influence on her personal faith journey. "I would never come back. I am very loyal to the faith community we have created, and I feel much a part of it. I love how immediate this community is; it is close to the earth. So I have faith in that group and am putting my eggs in that basket. If things were to evolve so that there is room for everyone at the table in the Church, I would certainly look at that. But I am not holding my breath on that occurring in my lifetime. I find myself listening to what Francis says. He truly is someone I look to for guiding me to be a better person and to have a better spiritual life. I am applying this to my daily life. But this is still not enough to bring me back to the Church. I consider myself Catholic, but not Roman Catholic."

For six of the twenty-one who had moved on, the response

was not so much "no" to the idea of returning to Catholicism but "perhaps" or "maybe" if the right changes took place. **Christina** commented, "The Catholic Church does matter to me. While acknowledging that I am still not practicing, what the pope says does matter to me now." The response from **Jamie** also showed a glimmer of hope, "I am very proud to be part of a Christianity where the pope is now part of the people, not above them or the 'I am in charge' sort of thing. This gives me faith in him."

Mark took it a step further, "For me, it has been a long time since I went to church. Some of the things Francis stands for give me hope, but I don't know if that has outweighed the frustrations I have. I do consider myself Catholic; it is a hard label to shake off. It was so much of my upbringing and family traditions, so attached to what I mean by family. But I haven't spent much time thinking about this. What would have to happen to attract me back to the Church? If I saw the Church use its resources to stand for justice for everyone, that would be a big start. I am a searcher who wants to be honest with my faith life and what I feel is right. I am optimistic about the possibilities, but like anyone who has been given an education in Catholic social justice, I am suspicious and skeptical. I am still a believer and believe in the Spirit—I would welcome the unexpected."

Jonathan is a searcher as well, "Has the pope had any influence on me? Yes and no. I don't go to church, and I'm not sure I would be considered a believer anymore, but I have been toying with going to church again. There is a parish in my neighborhood that I have been to a couple of times, and I actually enjoyed it the times that I went. With that background in mind, I don't think I look to the pope to be my spiritual leader, but looking at the messages he has been putting out, I look up to him as I might look up to the Dalai Lama. As a whole, the pope has not made that much difference to my own spiritual journey because I have not had much connection to him. It is not necessarily a too-late sort of thing regarding going back to the Church. I do, on occasion, attend a Catholic parish. I don't think that I have

closed that chapter of my life; it is just not something that I am
doing right now. There is a good parish close to my home that
does have a good community. I have attended the Sunday liturgy
there a few times. I am still trying to figure out my place in the
world and where I want to be, emotionally, spiritually, and with
other people, and things like that—I'm searching."

Theresa is a thoughtful person in her early sixties. She is con-
templating her next move, and Francis is part of her deliberations. "I am still watching the Church from the outside, but with
an emotional tie to the Church. I think what the pope has done
is making it easier for people to say, 'Yes, I'm Catholic.' They
can be proud of that. It doesn't have to have the negative bias it
had before Francis because it now has a little more affection and
a little more tenderness to it. It is easier to say you are Catholic
right out loud. No longer do I have to say, 'I won't be part of this
because they are hurting my brothers or sisters who are gay, or
who have had abortions, or who are divorced and remarried, or
have committed certain sins that don't allow them to come back
to church. So that makes a difference to me."

The Role of Women

The strongest reaction from those who no longer participate in
the life of the Church came in response to the role of women,
especially the priestly ordination issue. Two-thirds of those interviewed expressed a desire for women priests. This came from
eleven women, both young and old, and three men. **Christina**
commented, "I am not pleased with his statements about women.
This is disheartening. He seems to have closed the door on the
ordination of women. It was a jarring statement. I had hoped
for a turning of the corner on this one. He does foster a role for
women in the Church outside of ordination, perhaps as deacons."

Following up on that, **Diane** stated, "Francis looking into
women deacons is a start, and I don't know why I haven't seen
any results as yet. If that were to go through, it would be a start.

If I were the pope what would I do? I would say that women are equal in the sight of God and are able to serve in all aspects of liturgy and the hierarchy—the hierarchy would be much richer for it. I would bring in women who are good leaders and deep thinkers, ones who love the Church and want to be part of it. I would have half men and half women in positions of leadership. Those who have made the biggest difference in social justice I would bring in and put them in place."

Bridget was understanding of the slow pace of change, "Francis has not been the radical witness that I had hoped for around women's ordination. I don't think Francis is opposed to that, but I am not seeing his strides around this issue as I do with his work for the poor, or his emphasis on forgiveness and transparency. I also know that he is a product of his culture and his formation, so it is not surprising to me that women's ordination and the inclusion of women have not been his first priority. When I was doing ministry in the Catholic Church and was asked whether I thought the Church would ordain women, I would respond that the Catholic Church is one of *the* largest institutions on earth, and therefore, significant change has to take time because the Catholic Church is so vast and so complex. The fact that Francis has opened the door a crack is encouraging people to engage their conscience and use the pastoral forum for making decisions. I think this is absolutely appropriate for the Catholic Church."

Others were not so patient. Take **Susie**, for instance, "People say in general that the Roman Catholic Church is a world-wide church and it takes time. I want him to say, 'Two hundred years ago we negated slavery, and now I negate a two-party, two-tier system for men and women.' As pope, he can be prophetic. Be like Lincoln in pushing the right agenda, and take the risks in setting the agenda for emancipation of women in the Church. There must be some point for Francis where the awakening happens, a conversion takes place, an awareness of whose who are at the table and whose who are not at the table, or even in the

room. What is the problem about putting women's ordination
out there and let people react?"

Mary Jo was more emphatic: "Most disappointing to me
were his statements about not ordaining women and the role of
women in the Church. I think that was further reinforced when
he decided that maybe we could ordain married men, but would
not consider women. For me personally, it would be important
that he fully embrace the place of women in the Church, creating a system where there is equity and parity in the Church at
all levels. It is time to rip the bandaid off and ordain women.
I firmly believe God does not intend that the leadership of the
Catholic Church be all male. The male leadership has co-opted
the message and the institution." Colleen spoke in the same vein:
"I have always had issues with the Church. Number one, being
a woman and our place in the Catholic Church. The Church
is still exclusive, and it is going to hold on to not having any
women in power; the women's issue has not been dealt with."

Mark, a man in his early thirties, was very sympathetic
toward women's role in the Church. "I think when Francis came
in, a lot of people thought, 'Oh, he is a Jesuit, he is going to
flip the Church over; priests are going to be married and women
are going to be ordained and there will be marriage equality.'
He may seem radical in comparison with Pope Benedict, but I
don't think he is a revolutionary figure. But I think he is a step
in the right direction, for sure. I can't imagine how frustrating
it must be for women in the Church to have a group of men tell
them that the calling from God that they feel to the priesthood
is impossible. And there was not a woman in the room when
this discussion was held. To have an organization where all of
the power lies in the hands of only men, that's bad. If I were to
come in as pope and say, 'Women can be ordained,' this would
cause tremendous joy for one group and tremendous sadness for
another. If you want to keep the Church intact, the route would
be to call another Vatican Council and bring laity, both women
and men, to the table. Bring them all in and let them be part of

the decision making. Those who are saying that women can't be ordained have a broken view of men having some separate role from women, even better than the women. The fact that only men can have power in the Church is male supremacy."

Jonathan is another young man who struggles with the lack of movement on the ordination of women. "One of my greatest disappointments about Pope Francis has been his failure to move the Church forward on women's issues. I think that was what a lot of people were expecting, that he would move on women's issues and gay rights issues, and that the Church would be moving in a new direction. I think the Church has moved a bit because there is more emphasis on these issues, but the pope has made it clear that the Church is not going to have female priests anytime soon. That is disappointing. For a Church that is placing an emphasis on equality worldwide, it seems to be an inconsistent stance that only men can hold positions of leadership in the Church—this is obnoxious to me."

Highlights from Those on the Outside

What was learned from those who have moved out of the Catholic Church? Some of the key ideas included their attitude toward Francis, a shift in the issues the pope is emphasizing, the relationship between the pope and the institution, the extent to which these people might be interested in returning to the Catholic faith, and the role of women in the Church? These are the highlights:

- The people who have moved on said they like Francis and what he stands for, including his simpler lifestyle, his faith life centered on Jesus, his openness to all, no matter the person's religion, culture, status, orientation, or background. As **Andrew** mentioned, "He is more inclusive and open to all people being involved, all people no matter who they are." Those interviewed spoke of how this affected and challenged their own faith journey and way of acting.

- They also like the way Francis is shifting the focus and priorities of the Church away from an emphasis on rules and regulations and more toward attending to the pastoral and concrete needs of each individual, especially the poor and forgotten, the lonely and marginalized. "He could have all the power in the world," said **Bridget**, "but instead he is seeking solidarity with the poor of the world."

- Although this group of former Catholics was not as familiar with the institutional Church as were those who are still practicing, they experienced the pope as remaining independent enough to confront the self-aggrandizement and misuse of power associated with some of those who make up the hierarchy. **Nancy** realized how difficult this can be for a person in Francis's position. "I think he wants to be a free person, but all of the traditions get in the way."

- These people have left the Church for a variety of reasons, but one that has had a great impact is the inequality of women, especially in positions of leadership. A key component of that leadership is ordination. They find Pope Francis attractive as a human being and open to new ways of proceeding, but they would like him to at least allow a dialogue to begin around the requirements for the priesthood. "The pope is missing 50 percent of the population every time he has a conversation with only men—his confreres. That is what is holding us back," complained **Nancy**.

- One area that was not touched upon in this chapter is whether the present direction and new priorities laid out by Pope Francis will continue after he is no longer the pope. Predictions were mixed, both among those outside and those within the Church. Their responses will be included at the end of the next chapter.

Chapter 11

Proud to Be Called Catholic

This chapter contains the responses from the thirty-one people who, although less active in parish and Church involvement in 2012 than they once were, still called themselves Catholic and members of the Church. When asked in 2017 whether Pope Francis had made a difference to them, they replied in a sentiment similar to what **Kristy** had to say: "Francis is giving me hope—I love the way he does things. It goes back to the way Jesus would do things. He is very simple, very focused, in tune with the people—he discards a lot of the hoopla that is in the Vatican. I think Francis is terrific."

Proud to Be Catholic

Those who have decided to remain Catholic are even more enthusiastic about Pope Francis than those who have moved on. The sadness they felt about the direction of the Church suddenly turned into joy. **Phillip** admitted, "I was so discouraged. I kept asking myself, 'Where are we going; why are we going so far backward?' Then came Francis—what a breath of fresh air!"

This same reaction was repeated throughout the interviews of those remaining in the Church. An important juncture had been reached and things were beginning to change. **Jane** called it a pivot. "I am proud now of the pope and of the Church. There has been a pivot that has been made, and it is an important pivot." **Anne** described it as regaining trust. "He renews my hope and

my trust. My anger toward the Church has mellowed because of
Pope Francis." **Ed** put it in a historical context. "The selection
of Francis was what I was praying for without knowing it. This
election liberated me in the sense that I went back to the euphoria I experienced during the three or four years of the Vatican II
Council in the 1960s. Everything about this guy reminded me
of how Pope John XXIII had a similar but briefer affect on my
thinking and my compass." The feelings of euphoria and hope
came from all quarters. **Allyson** exclaimed, "It is hard not to
be proud of Pope Francis as our leader. It is encouraging that
people you love and respect, who have been negative and critical
of the faith in the past, are now saying, 'Wow, that Pope Francis
is amazing.' Or 'I love that guy,' and they aren't even Catholic.
That makes me feel good; that makes me feel empowered. He
has a global reach, no matter who the people might be."

What is it about this pope that is so attractive, that fosters such
positive reactions? A humble manner and a simple lifestyle are
two attributes. **Kathleen** described it this way: "Characteristics
of Pope Francis that stand out: his humility, his willingness to
step away from all of the traditional trappings of the papacy, his
understanding of people from the poor to the wealthy. His willingness to walk where the people are. His joy and happiness are
very evident to me." **Greg** agreed. "His personal actions and his
expression of spirituality has inspired me. It is interesting that he
is a Jesuit, but it is more of a miracle that he is a *humble* Jesuit.
What impressed me is that he is a servant leader." **Pam** saw it as
being personable and accessible. "He just seems like someone
you would want to walk up to and talk to." **Richard** summed
up Francis's simple lifestyle by stating, "He understands symbol-
ism—making some key gestures, such as washing the feet of the
poor, living in a humble apartment, driving himself in his little
car, no fancy dress or red shoes."

According to those interviewed, being open to everyone was
another strong hallmark of Francis's way of acting. When asked
what was memorable about the pope, **Kerry** mentioned, "His

acceptance of people different from himself is impressive. He is a man of integrity and consistency—his actions match the words he uses. People have a great sense of love for him. Disaffected Catholics, non-Catholics, and people of no faith are drawn to him and his message." **Danielle** described this openness to others in very human terms. "I can't tell you how much I appreciate that man. When he was in the popemobile and he was riding around, he was laughing, and smiling, and waving. You could tell he was soaking up the energy of the people."

Rachael was finishing college when Francis stepped out onto the balcony. "I do remember when Pope Francis got elected—my friends and I were seniors in college at the time and on spring break. We were sitting on a beach and, like good Catholics, we knew the election was happening. Someone yelled, 'There's white smoke, there's white smoke!' So we ran in to see the news, and we were shocked that he was a Jesuit. We said, 'What?!' I will never forget that. Even people who are not in the religious bubble know who he is. That has been a positive shift, especially in light of the sex abuse scandals and ongoing shifts that have happened in the Church. I really like him and think he is a really holy person. His image is of a jolly man, clearly filled with joy and light."

Others recognized the pope's keen intelligence and astuteness, along with a deep spirituality. **Rachael** described him as being "politically savvy." **Ginny** stressed his religious background by stating, "The fact that he is a Jesuit, with Jesuit spirituality and contemplative practice that I am aware of, and skills for discerning the Spirit, are very, very important in his office. I don't think we have had this before with the previous popes. He seems to be a good listener. Again, this is something that is very valued and needed in the Church. He is not afraid to speak the Gospel to the world—particularly when the world needs a Gospel witness of values. That has been very encouraging to me." **Phillip** called him "a very bright man, a very faith-filled man; a person who is willing to listen, a person who is willing to see all sides of an issue. In particular, there is an opportunity to look forward, to question, to be open to dialogue."

Evidence of his intelligence is found in his way of leading. As **John** described it, "He is an exceptionally kind individual, which is not often associated with leadership and can be seen as a weakness. He is very self-assured, but without any sense of arrogance." **Kathleen** commented, "His Jesuit background shows me that he has a good intellectual foundation and that shows in what he does and says. He is not afraid of walking down the streets in Rome. He is not afraid of dying, as if he were saying, 'What have I got to lose?'"

New Directions

From the first moment Francis was elected pope he set the Church in a new direction. He challenged many long-held traditions and created a new set of priorities, and he did this across a wide spectrum. A shift began the moment he was elected and asked the waiting crowd to pray for him. More changes followed, including a new emphasis on the poor and marginalized, a strong pastoral approach focused on people's individual experiences rather than "one size fits all," calling into question clericalism and privilege among those in leadership positions, stressing care for the world's environment and the links this has with the way the poor are treated, a new transparency that led to the way the Vatican Bank did its business, a fresh concentration on the example and teachings of Jesus. These are some of the ways in which Francis was changing the direction of the Church. As **Richard** said, "He has not changed Church rules but has gone about it in a different way. He has created a good image for the Catholic Church."

Some of those interviewed praised the pope for making any changes at all. **Anne** found this exhilarating, "The change that has happened with Pope Francis is allowing questions to be asked and delegating lay leaders to solve the problems and provide the answers. A new momentum is starting up! A new world is dawning." A similar sentiment came from **Allyson**. "He is presenting the Church in a new way that we have not seen for a while." **Phillip** felt the changes Francis initiated got people fired up and eager to try out new ways of acting. "The thing that gives me hope is that people seem to be more alive in their faith, and this is because of Francis. People are now more energized to continue working in the Church." In more graphic terms, **Paul** described the impact Francis's changes have had on people. "Once in a while he throws a firecracker onto the playground and this causes people to jump, but it's not so bad that they run screaming from the schoolyard." He does seem to get people's attention, in other words.

Those who were interviewed mentioned concrete ways that Francis was changing the status quo. One was paying attention to the poor and finding concrete ways to meet their needs. More than one person mentioned the showers for the homeless and other services to meet their needs that he added in the Vatican. **Jane** remarked, "The one thing I love above anything else is that Francis put in the laundromat for the homeless in the Vatican. That was so very practical—a place where they could wash their clothes. But this was hugely symbolical for me. The reason I think it is so symbolic is that there really is a huge divide between people who have plenty and those who don't. If you have plenty and are in a certain social/economic group, you don't know those people who have nothing, and you don't see those people, except out on the road with a sign asking for help. I think it was the pope who said, 'If you give these people something, look them in the eye—don't give it to them and hurry by.' That struck me." **Danielle** mentioned the same thing. "I am more hopeful for our Church now. He has put showers in the Vatican for the homeless; he has opened it up so they can get haircuts and shaves. He has brought refugees into the Vatican, saying, 'We have rooms for them here.'"

Francis's emphasis on climate change was also a new direction. **Barbara** exclaimed, "There are so many things about him that are so good. His awareness of climate change and the horrible damage done to the environment and the need to work at changing it." **Maureen** felt the same way. "I am so grateful that we got him. His Synod on the Family—I loved that. And the environment too—*Laudato Si'*. Those are the things I would commend him for. He has given us a new vision."

Taking people as they are rather than how you would like them to be was another new direction initiated by the pope. **Richard** commented, "He did say that based on one's conscience, irregular unions have lots of love in them. People who are divorced and remarried are not excommunicated. This makes me feel better about my children in such relationships. He stimulated lots of discussions in many areas. The pope is inspiring people to be more spiritual despite not going to church. I feel better because of him. I don't have to be defensive in talking about the divorced and remarried, making personal conscience decisions, people living together and not married, and birth control issues."

Encouraging priests and people alike to get out of their comfort zone and "hit the streets" was a strong new direction. **Ed** was excited by what he had read and seen of the pope. "My goodness, this guy has really got it—he is teaching us in every single move he makes—washing the feet on that first Holy Thursday, and everything after. His speeches are consistent: Get out of the church, get out of the sacristy, and get out into the streets and get with the people, especially the people who are hurting. That is what he is doing. The good shepherd is going out looking for the lost sheep. Francis is bringing us back to what the Vatican Council said—we have to be in touch with the world; we can't be closed up, we cannot be building walls (bridges, not walls)—he is very consistent about that." **Jane** said the same. "The thing I love is that he said the Church should be a field hospital. That was the vision of Jesus. I have faith and confidence that the Spirit will move in and sometimes upend things and get everybody back on the right track."

Making the Church more relevant was the new direction **Tom** emphasized. "My children and grandchildren and friends now see the Church as a little more realistic, a little more flexible, a little less rigid. These people are coming to realize that the Church is changing. Morals do not change, but situations do. That is why I say the pope has brought in more flexibility. The view of some of my kids and many of my friends had been that the Church has been increasingly removed from modern realities and anxieties. Francis has brought up the fact that we are just humans; we are not perfect and life is challenging. We still have moral obligations, but we can use human consciousness to still make moral judgments. It was always there, but the pope has certainly brought up the plight of the poor. In light of the unemployed and immigration, Francis has brought it forward."

Kathleen agreed. "Instead of Church leaders who were standing so self-righteously, this pope has given us a Church that is more flexible, more understanding of life as it actually is for most people. His insights and insightfulness are profound. His words to the U.S. Congress were supportive. He spoke of the need for them to make it their business to listen to all of their people and hear their words, and then have the courage to legislate well. 'You Congress people,' he said, 'need to deal with courage in serving your people, not from the political side but for the good of humanity.' He is not afraid of any of these situations. I would be happy to approach him—it would be a real thrill. I guess that when I tell people that when we saw the pope and waved to him as he drove by, it was not his popeness that was a thrill to me, but to see a man who was like any other person—a real human being."

Dealing with the Hierarchy

Chapter 10 reported on how those who have left the Church responded when asked whether Pope Francis was the same as or different from the institution. Attitudes were mixed. For those who have remained Catholic the issue was more about what influence the pope has had on the hierarchy. As **Caroline** put it, "In the beginning when he became pope, I really felt he was different from the institution because he made so many outright statements against the hierarchy and didn't want to wear all of the fancy robes and ruby slippers and such. When you come up against a lot of flak or have to deal with a lot of pressure, it can make one pull back if you are not a solid-enough person. I am hoping he is solid enough that he will not be swayed in that regard. I still remain hopeful that he is a rock-solid person and that his beliefs will be strong enough to have people stop and pay attention."

A number of people spoke of the pushback that Francis must be experiencing in dealing with some of those in the hierarchy. Joanne gave credit to the pope for the way he was handling this. "I think it has been interesting to watch the Vatican intrigue and the shenanigans coming from a band of cardinals who were criticizing the pope. He seems to have good humor in managing that. He does not show it if they are getting under his skin; this is a good thing. Trying to move the Vatican bureaucracy is so hard—I don't know whether anyone is capable of that." She went on to say, "I hope the pope can appoint good men as bishops and cardinals, ones who see the reality of the situation and are not taken up with the trappings of their office. That is what is so important. If you are a bishop living in the lap of luxury, you are not living in reality. I think he is trying to be countercultural, and I am grateful for that and cheer him on. When I hear him speak against clericalism and the evil of clericalism, I appreciate that. Francis is so quick to talk about the shepherd smelling like the sheep. This is overdue and it makes the bishops squirm. The Catholic Church had very antiquated views, but Francis has made the Gospel relevant again. The Church has frittered away much of its moral authority with the child abuse situation."

Maureen cheered him on, stating, "I think that Francis has done a wonderful job with the calling he has received, which I feel is cleaning house from the bottom up. There is a great need for this because, with any institution, it tends to be taken over by those in power. He definitely has a wider vision than the bishops and cardinals, and not just because he is the pope. Francis is a very big threat to change as far as the clergy is concerned. I am very happy with the bishops he has appointed. I think that is where the hope is going to be. That makes me very hopeful."

Kathleen picked up on his recent appointments but added that he has made some good "de-appointments" as well. "What he has to say is closer to the way I would like to perceive the Church, as generous, loving, pastoral, and minimizing the rules, getting back down to the few dogmas we have to have. He does want to get rid of that high-powered superiority that is part of many of those in the hierarchy. He has made some good appointments of bishops and archbishops recently. This pope is very politically savvy. He just is not afraid—of the hierarchy, of the poor, of the reckless or felons. He is not afraid to fire people or put them in positions that have little power. He is not afraid to confront, but not confront harshly. You get the impression that when people are moved out, he seems to do it so gently, saying, 'It is time for you to move on.'"

Asking people to move on was not always well received. Claudia commented, "Talk about a culture shock when Francis became the pope. Trying to right this Church is like trying to turn an ocean liner in a big ocean.—Wow, that's hard. He must be getting it from all sides. It doesn't seem to get to him, though. His real job is to fulfill the mission of the Church, which is to help people become more prayerful, become more inclusive, more like Jesus, and help people get to heaven. This is what I think he lives for, not for the institution. The forces that he is up against are so caught up in the institution, but Francis has been able to stay focused and see the things that have to change. He prayerfully has the courage of his convictions."

"He is bucking the institution," said Phillip, "and I applaud him for this because I feel the institution needs to be pushed. My dream for the structure is, instead of top down and trickle down, make it more comprehensive, make it more democratic. I think he is edging that way with his council, his confidants, his kitchen cabinet. I'm a Catholic and I'll always be a Catholic, but I had to form my own separate peace with certain aspects of the hierarchy under the formal Church. Francis certainly is a sound and faithful representative of the Roman Catholic Church, but I think his paradigm of the Church is moving past a medieval paradigm. I think the medieval paradigm of the Catholic Church still holds a lot of sway—the structure, the behavior, the manner of thinking. He has a much simpler approach to Church, more focused on mercy and love. He has a job to do, and I think he takes it very seriously. I hope that everything that surrounds him, the structure and all that, will carry it forward. I think he has changed the emphasis for those who want to hear it. There are others who do not like him and are waiting for him to die and have someone more 'sensible' to come in. I think that is always the way things will be." On the other hand, as **Dan** mentioned, "Francis is not bashful about letting his agenda be known, as with the pre-Christmas talk to the Curia a few years after his election that was against clericalism and careerism."

On the positive side of Francis's dealings with the hierarchy, there is the situation of finding priests to staff parishes in outlying areas. **Ed** remarked, "I like the story about the Brazilian bishop who has an enormous geographic territory and only a handful of priests. This bishop asked, 'Holy Father, I would like to ordain indigenous, married catechists.' And the pope said, 'I would like to do that, too. You go build a consensus in your country among the national bishops of Brazil and then something can happen.' I think that after a certain amount of time that could happen."

Influence on the Individual

Did Pope Francis have any direct influence on the individual person, one that did not come by way of the local parish or religious programs? Some said that they were changed and others not so much. For instance, **Kristy** said, "There has been no change in my behavior as a Catholic because of Pope Francis—I have always been a liberal Catholic." **Maureen** mentioned, "My own views have not changed because of him, although Francis has made me feel much better about the faith." **Tom** added, "For me personally, having Francis as the pope has not changed me. Other than that, I am happy about it, so I suppose that has influenced me. Indirectly, it has affected me because it has given me ammunition in talking with other people. Because he is like a ray of light; that is a positive change for me."

The one who expressed the least influence was **Leah**. When first interviewed, she was graduating from college and still an active Catholic. In recent years she has pulled away from the Church. In her words, "He has not made a huge impact on me regarding the Church over the last four years or so. I still have the same understanding of God and creation and still have the same understanding of myself and my purpose in the world as I did when I was in college and very close to the Catholic Church. But it just works differently now and is expressed differently. Where does the pope fit into all of this? Barely. Pope Francis has not been entirely out of my scope, but he has been far off the radar. Occasionally some news from a Catholic news organization or some of my friends or family members who are pretty Catholic will post to me, 'Francis said this, or did this today.' To be honest, I don't feel strongly one way or the other—I'm pretty neutral. I haven't been impacted by his time as pope because that stuff is not reaching me through my news system."

For others, it was a "yes and no" sort of thing. **Kerry** admitted, "Not so much practices, but I do have more hope moving forward. When Francis says that he is following the Gospel of Jesus, I try to do that also. So I think he makes a difference to me because I am more positive about the Church than I was before he was elected, especially the direction the Church is going." A similar comment came from **Anne**. "I am no different from where I was in 2011, but now I feel a need for urgency. I am in a position of influence, so I want to use it as best I can, not for power over others, but power for change, just like the pope is doing. I am getting reconnected and participating more. One way is through simple thoughts to help with everyday work and experiences. These thoughts are based on the corporal and spiritual works of mercy. What can we do in Francis's image to be helpful to people? Do simple things, one-on-one. Say something nice to people. This makes such a difference. Remember to do it each day—bring this to daily prayer. Follow the example of the pope in taking the bus. Walk the streets!"

Others were much more emphatic that he did affect change in their lives. **Danielle** related, "He challenges me to open up my eyes beyond my community and look out to the world, stand up for immigrants and refugees, open up the front door and let people into my life because for some reason the Spirit has sent these people to me. Francis is giving me an example personally." The pope also changed **Denise's** way of operating. "The pope's affect on me? It has given me a little more hope to provide a home for homeless youth, a group home for teenagers. This goes back to Francis going out to the less fortunate. I am calmer, not as angry toward the institutional Church as I was before Francis's election. Before that I was ready to shove the whole Church thing."

For **Fayann**, the pope did not change her beliefs but her values and ways of acting. "He seems to be somebody that I can identify with in terms of values for the earth and values for openness to one another and the value of not judging others but listening to them. In those ways he has challenged me. He is engaged in the world, and that challenges me to continue to be engaged in the world as well. He is a positive influence and not a judger. How am I different now? I feel that there is an openness with Pope Francis that creates the possibility for surprises."

It was the pope's attitude toward the poor that changed **John's** perceptions. "Francis's notion is that we have to learn from the poor. That struck me as being a unique sort of wisdom. We tend to look down on the poor as not our intellectual equals, and we equate what we have learned in our schools and from our families as 'wisdom.' But Francis has taken a different track in addressing that issue. He has made a difference to me because I feel that now I can look at the Church with a greater sense of possibilities. The pope has made me more comfortable with my faith journey because he is focused more on the human side of our existence and how all share more in common than how we differ from one another. Francis has reinforced some of my views and made me more comfortable with some of the things I struggle with."

For **Tony**, it was the pope's approach to Christian living and his spirituality of "letting go" that influenced him. "Before Francis, practicing my faith was getting a laundry list prepared and then doing those things one at a time. I am struggling with that now—the laundry list is not the same thing for me anymore. I am not sure what it is or what it will be—I am in the middle of a transition. Being less shallow is what I want it to be. What he has done for me is given me a lot of good examples, and those things have had an effect on me more than I realize. Francis shows me the way. I am now asking, 'What's next Lord?' The pope is telling us that God is greater than we ever imagined. I like Francis's openness, and I wish I could be the same way. He has priorities, and they are all very pastoral and relational. In the past I was so sure of everything. I am no longer there. It is a letting go now. This is part of the hope and trust of Francis. Francis is so decentralized—getting us, in practical ways, out of our comfort zones. I am learning how to be very, very patient."

For **Allyson**, it was new hope and more confidence. "I just hope I can live up to what he stands up for and what he has done. I don't think Francis has changed my views of my own faith, but he has given me more confidence to live my Catholic faith, to hold up my head as a Catholic. It has made me want to share what he says with other people. My own judgment of people is more pastoral now—I try to hear their story rather than be critical; how can I make it easier for them. I am greeting people on my walks more—engaging people in conversation. The pope does this, and it motivates me to do the same. I do feel connected to him because he is doing it, and there are a lot of people now doing it besides him. I relate to world situations more now. I am certain there is an element there that comes from the pope. I do feel connected to him. I am sure that if I encountered him at the front door, I would ask him to come in before I would think about how remarkable this is. What to ask him? First of all, I would ask him to put his hand on my head and bless me. I would not ask him anything—the conversation would just go on. He might ask about my life—he is a good listener."

Paul also wanted to interact with the pope in a familiar setting. "He is the kind of guy I would like to sit with and enjoy dinner and a glass of wine, where as with Benedict I would be afraid whether the forks are straight and did I spill on the tablecloth." Paul went on to add, "Francis has influenced me to become a much better Christian. I am volunteering in Church-related areas and with Catholic college students. I might even try to put together a pilgrimage to the Holy Land."

Claudia not only had a change of heart because of Francis, she started coming back to the Eucharist as well. "Was I feeling good about Francis? Yes, I was. When he was elected pope, I was still searching for the right place to go to church. Like a whole lot of other people I talked to, I was wishing that he had come along sooner. I can't tell you how many people told me, 'I would not have left the Church if he had become the pope earlier.' And I say, 'But he *was* made pope, and now look at the hope he brings.' But these people are not coming back to the Church. Nor was I ready to come back when he was first elected—I was still very angry. I have now been going to church regularly for the last six months. It took a long time for me to get to this point. Francis made a difference to me. I feel I am at a crossroad now. I am very prayerful about what God wants me to do next. I feel like another journey is just about to begin for me. I have to find a place where I can make a difference."

Will It Continue?

The question is, "Will the shift Francis has created and the direction he has initiated endure once he is no longer the pope?" From those who have left the Church, not many had much to offer. Diane was afraid that he was taking too many risks in being so available and open to the public. "He does not protect himself, he doesn't have guards, he doesn't live in a palace, he goes out to do works of mercy. I could see him getting bumped off." She went on to ask, "Will his legacy continue after he is gone?" and then offered this dire prediction: "If it doesn't, it will become a very extreme religion, and I don't see much hope for the world."

On a happier note, **Mary Jo** commented, "The good news is that the cardinals and bishops he is choosing now are much more open and like-minded to Francis. Whether or not there will be enough of them not to reverse course when Francis retires or dies is unknown. Maybe they will be frightened by what Francis has done in opening the doors and they will backtrack, I don't know." **Mark** found hope in how Francis was elected and that it could happen again. "I was very surprised that the cardinals chose to elect him and that Benedict chose to resign—that was unheard of. I hope that the humility he brings to the office will continue. I hope he can impact the institution in some way. I think he has a vision for justice and for change, so I would like to imagine he is stacking the deck with a group of cardinals in order to keep it going and have a lasting impact."

Many more of those who have remained Catholic than those who have moved on offered insights into what the future might hold. It was a serious issue for them because the direction of their own religion was at stake. When asked, "Will it continue?" **Pam** responded, "I don't want to think about that. I hope he is around long enough that his thoughts become the norm so we do get someone who is like-minded to him. I think it will continue in this direction, but I could be so naïve."

Phillip finds hope in the way Francis has been operating thus far. "He is so long-range in his thinking and the people he is appointing. He has a vision, and he wants this vision to continue after he is gone. I sure hope the Holy Spirit is around when Francis decides to retire or he dies. It is certainly obvious that the Spirit is here now." **Rachael** also mentioned the power of the Spirit at work. "Will his direction continue when he is gone? I don't know, but the Spirit is moving. The Spirit cannot be held back. Will the Church keep changing or is this just temporary— the jury is still out about that."

According to **Larry**, it all depends on the cardinals doing the electing. "If he retires or passes on, I don't have a lot of confidence on who the next person might be or that he will pick up the banner of Pope Francis. Except the pope is elected by the cardinals, and if you get all of your candidates lined up you can get something done. If you can't get them lined up, you are going to be out of luck for a long time. I don't know how many people are with Francis or how the pendulum has swung, but I have a sense that it is swinging. I would hope that this would be the case and that it continues on the upswing." **Claudia** also mentioned the swing of a pendulum and had hope in the end result. "Will this Francis-effect continue after he dies? I have to believe that, despite the resistance against the pendulum swinging the other way, the same cardinals who voted him in will keep this going. They knew whom they were putting into office, and they have got to realize that changes are needed if the faith and strength of the Catholic Church will be sustainable. I'm hoping this will happen."

Kathleen was more emphatic about the hopes she had for the future. "Will this trend continue? I feel completely that Francis is the work of the Holy Spirit. I also believe, because I like him and agree with him, that I have a conviction that the popes are chosen with the cooperation of the Spirit; this one especially so because it was so unlikely. Besides, when he dies, he will be in a position to influence the election of the next pope. For all we know, Francis may step down like Benedict did, but he will be himself, no matter how old he gets." **John** felt that no matter who is chosen as the next pontiff, part of the spirit that Francis initiated will continue. "It would not be unusual for there to be a step back from what he has gotten started. I would be hopeful that even though Francis may not be able to change the institution, that the people within the institution would change, that is, the faithful. That part will not be undone when he departs."

Highlights from Those Who Remain Catholic

Some of the key findings from the interviews of those who have remained members of the Catholic Church include the following:

- These Catholics were pleased with the election of Pope Francis. They felt they could raise their heads high and announce, "I am a Catholic and I am proud of it," without fear of ridicule or recrimination. This was true, no matter the environment or religious leanings of those interviewed. As **Kristy** exclaimed, "A pope like this only comes along once in a lifetime. Lots of people on Facebook just love him—people of all faiths and backgrounds."

- There was no doubt in the minds of almost all of the Catholics interviewed that Francis has mapped out a new path to follow that included new priorities and emphases. His breadth of vision is wide and all inclusive, ranging from care for the poor and marginalized to making room for diverse and imperfect lifestyles, from the environment to clericalism, from making room for everyone to financial transparency. "Because of Francis," said **Danielle**, "more people are speaking up for greater inclusiveness, saying, 'Let's collaborate more.' I see the Church opening up its doors even wider than what they have been."

- People's perception of the interchange between Pope Francis and the hierarchy was telling. Because he is single-minded in confronting clericalism and lavish lifestyles, he has ruffled the feathers of those in positions of power and control. As a result he is experiencing criticism and pushback. But those interviewed cheer him on for his efforts and want him to stay strong and continue to steer a course of renewal and reform of the institution. **Anne** admitted, "I am regaining my trust in him and in the Church. Some bishops are still doing naughty things, while others like him. Change the culture! Build in an accountability structure." That is what Francis seems to be doing.

• Pope Francis has cut through the bureaucracy and has appealed directly to ordinary people, both Catholics and those of other religions, whatever their station in life may be. Many people are taking this to heart and are changing their way of thinking and acting. **Barbara** was one such person. "I see him challenging me to be better, to constantly be growing in my spiritual journey. I like that challenge and I don't feel threatened by it."

• Will Francis's legacy continue after he is no longer the pope? As **Rachael** put it, "The jury is still out about that." But most of those interviewed hope that this would happen and were optimistic that with the help of the Holy Spirit and a critical mass of favorable cardinals at the next conclave, that the present momentum and current priorities spelled out by Francis will endure, and that the pendulum will continue to swing in the present direction. **Danielle**, in response to the question, "Will it continue?" replied, "When I look at who this last batch of cardinals appointed by Francis were, I have more hope for the Church. I really do."

Chapter 12

The Ordination Issue

In many countries around the world there is a critical shortage of priests to staff local parishes, to provide leadership, administer the sacraments, serve the needs of the faithful and those seeking help. One solution would be to allow married men to be ordained to the priesthood. For over half of the Church's history this was permitted. Even now, exceptions are being made for Episcopal priests who are married to join the Church and function as Catholic priests in good standing.

Pope Francis has encouraged the Brazilian bishops to discuss this issue for certain outlying areas where the shortage of priests is acute. An article by John Phillips appeared in the London *Telegraph* on November 2, 2017, stating, "Pope Francis has requested a debate over allowing married men in the Amazon region of Brazil to become priests. The pontiff made the decision to put a partial lifting of priestly celibacy up for discussion and a possible vote by the Brazilian bishops following a request made by Cardinal Claudio Hummes, the president of the bishops' commission for the Amazon. Cardinal Hummes reportedly asked Francis to consider ordaining so-called *viri probati*, married men of great faith, capable of ministering spiritually to the many remote communities in the Amazon where there is a shortage of priests, and evangelical Christians and pagan sects are displacing Catholicism."

Both those who have left Catholicism and those who remain saw little difficulty with this shift in the requirements for ordination to include men who are married. Where they did express concern was not allowing the ordination of women to the priest-hood. Chapter 10 reported on the feelings of those who have moved out of the Church (see "The Role of Women," p. 98). Eleven out of the twenty-one former Catholics who were inter-viewed, both men and women, expressed their opinions on this issue. Some of them were conciliatory, expressing the need to proceed with caution, while others voiced their strong desire to allow women to be ordained to the priesthood. For **Diane,** for instance, it was the one issue that determined her decision to remain outside of the Catholic faith. "I would never come back because of the Church's stance on women—I just never would come back because of that."

There were also strong opinions on this issue among those who have remained Catholic. Twenty-six out of thirty-one touched upon this topic. Because of this strong showing, it requires a sep-arate chapter. Attitudes covered a wide range of feelings, from thinking this was a bad idea, to those who would like Pope Fran-cis to make the decision favoring women's ordination right now. **Allyson,** who was against having women priests, still thought they should be included in the important decisions facing the Church. "I don't think women should be priests—none of that. But there is still a place for women in the Church to be leaders, to have a place of some decision-making power. That should be respected. We have all been given intelligence and compassion. Women use it just as well as men, so that should be respected."

Pam, although favoring women's ordination, had a pessimis-tic view about whether it would ever come about. "I don't think women's ordination will ever happen, so I have a fatalistic opin-ion on this. I have now stopped thinking about it. The pope's reaction to women deacons and his openness to look into this is positive. Yes, he has done a lot in this respect. I just think it will never happen. But I would like it if he did make this change and allow women to be ordained."

Danielle thought that the pope was already doing a number of things to include women in important positions of influence and leadership. "I feel that Francis has opened the doors of the institution to women so much more than what was done before. Just take the Vatican, for instance. He has put more women in positions of prominence since he has been there. I was extremely interested in reading about how the Vatican has opened up more to women working there in prominent roles. For instance, one of the women working there is now the director of the Vatican Museum. The fact that Francis has a study group on the women's diaconate is huge. This would never have come about with the popes we have had previously. So I see him respecting women more; I see him acknowledging women in what they are capable of doing and the work that they do within their own churches and in the universal Church. Women's ordination is a big deal, but Francis will not be able to do it. I see the diaconate for women happening before the ordination of women, and married men being ordained before these other two."

The pope forming a study group on ordaining women for the diaconate was mentioned by many as a good step in the right direction. **Greg** contended, "I think this is a seminal issue for the Church. Francis himself has made some statements. He certainly doesn't see women being ordained as priests, although he has opened the door for the discussion about women becoming deacons. The deaconate is Holy Orders. There are degrees of Holy Orders: deacon, priest, bishop. In his actions, he presents himself as very open, but he is not making radical statements that women should have as full a role in the Church as men have. I think he even referred to Pope John Paul II's statement that this is basically a closed issue—we should not be discussing this. But if women would be admitted to the permanent deaconate, wouldn't that be a pretty strong step that we need to continue to look at women's role in the Church? I would see that as a pretty strong step. Whether that will be effective, I don't know. I would like to see him move the Church forward in terms of a stronger, wider voice and a change in the roles for women in the Church. Would I like to see it? Yes."

Ordaining women to the priesthood would be a very big step for the Catholic Church. Many of those interviewed felt that it was a worthy goal to shoot for, but counseled that moving slowly would bring good results in the end. **Jane** cautioned, "It is wonderful that Francis has done the things that he has, but when is he going to address this issue of ordination? I understand this attitude, but I think, little by little, these changes are going to have to be made incrementally. I wish it was not like that, but realistically I think it is. Francis has made some movement by allowing a study on women deacons and married men being ordained for rural areas. The women issue is also part of a bigger picture—it is not the Church's fault that it is the way it is—women are not treated fairly in the larger world. I think that Francis, being a very bright man, along with everything else, realizes that he is in this position, but he has to move at a pace that will be accepted by his colleagues. He has to go at a slower pace because he would get too much pushback from the Curia and conservative members of the faithful if he made sudden changes. There are very conservative Catholics who were just fine with the way things were and are uneasy with Pope Francis. The first step would be to admit women to the diaconate."

Kathleen was losing patience. "I would like to know why he is not ordaining women. Is it something about women or about the mood of the populace? Would it do harm to the Church? Why would that be a problem? We have women priests in the Episcopal Church who are doing a spectacular job and, in that case, are not pushing out the men. He might leave this issue until after Pope Benedict XVI dies; that would create a new situation."

Barbara stressed what the positive effects would be if Francis took the risk to make such a change. "Francis could have such a wonderful impact on the whole world if he would take a stand on women. It would take tremendous courage, and I know he would find so much resistance from so many of the hierarchs around him. It is probably inconceivable that he could say something that would insist on the equality of men and women made in the image of God. But it could make such a difference, not to just the Church but to the whole world, if the Catholic Church, with its billion people membership, would take an official stand on the true equality of women and men. It would make such a difference. It would be truly revolutionary if the pope were to write something along that line of equality that would have a similar impact as *Laudato Si'* is having."

Denise also saw the advantages of a shift in this direction. "We need to look at how we can regenerate or change the concept of priesthood. It needs to be a broader term; there need to be ways of bringing more people into priesthood. We can't exclude women from priesthood anymore. Francis is talking about women deacons. This is a first step, but there needs to be action, not just talk or sound bites. It is hard to believe that priests would be afraid about their jobs being taken away, although women in most parishes today really run and are integral to the administration of the Church. However, with the impending priest shortage, maybe the priests are worried they will become just Mass-machines. The main issue now is the shortage of priests and not enough priestly or religious vocations. It is time to think more inclusively and creatively, as well as eliminating the clerical power trips of the hierarchy. Perhaps we should go back to the early model of the Church in the first century."

The issue of women's ordination may also be related to one's culture and background. That was what **Ed** brought up in his interview. "A woman in our community came up to me after I mentioned some of these matters and said, 'But I cannot get over what he is doing to women, or *not* doing. How he misses that point.' I said, 'I am with you, but we are dealing with a guy who is a product of his own machismo culture.' She said in reply, 'I suppose,' but she said it with resignation. Regarding women, I think it is more cultural; it is in his bones."

Joanne raised the same issue of his background. "Francis's attitudes toward women are troubling. I try to remember that this is an eighty-plus-year-old, celibate man who is coming from

Latin American and has an Italian background. You can only expect so much from him and from his attitudes toward women. But that issue does trouble me. I like the fact that he is willing to have a discussion about women deacons. Many think this could be a slippery slope to ordination. I can see how this could be very threatening to the hierarchy. I am not one of those persons who says that if we had married priests and women priests we would not have problems. Both of those things would create a whole different set of problems. But it would be a healthier situation for the human beings involved. The Church is going to make itself irrelevant if it doesn't pay attention to what is going on here. For those of us who are ontologically inadequate (women), there is not much room for us to serve in the Church in a meaningful way—we can only be the handmaidens, but no more. But I have to be hopeful and believe that the Spirit is still working in the Church. If I believe that, then God will not abandon the people. We have that promise, and we have to hang on to that."

Fayann was also discouraged by the pope's stance on women's ordination, but she saw both negative and positive aspects to the pope's cultural and religious background. "I believe that women should be included much more in the Church. Not only are women well prepared with knowledge, but Jesus himself had women followers—many of them. It was the women who stuck with him to the end. It was the women who comforted his mother. I am very disappointed that the pope reaffirmed that there will be no women priests." She then reflected on Francis's background as part of the reason he is holding back on this, but also how it might prove helpful. "It does not seem to be a strong suit of his from what I have read. Francis comes out of a Latin American reality. But he is listening to women religious and to women in general. The fact that he has agreed to have theologians look at the question of the ordination of women to the diaconate is a very positive step—for me at least it is. However, since he is a Jesuit, the women's issue has more of a chance because he knows the importance of discernment of spirits and how you have to listen to both sides of the issue and not skew the conversation to make sure it agrees with you. And you don't have people giving you feedback who only share your ecclesiology or your theology, but you are open to everyone you have asked to study the question. That gives me reason to hope that it is going to be a more legitimate discernment of the Spirit and is not going to be skewed."

Tony was also encouraged by the pope's careful process of discernment. "He has opened himself to seeing new things. Who knows whether he will see the women's thing differently. It may not be his priority right now but it may become so later." **Caroline** also took a wait-and-see attitude. "I think there are so many things the Catholic Church could change or do better. One thing is, I think, that they should allow women to be ordained and serve in that capacity as well. I don't know whether the pope is in favor of ordaining women or not—I have not heard that statement made. He is very open to women in supportive roles, but how far that goes we will have to wait and see how much he can make things happen."

What follows are the stories of two young women, both of whom were graduating from college when first interviewed. They now have taken different paths regarding membership in the Church and had different ways of responding to the pope's approach to women's ordination. First, **Leah**. "I think my disillusionment started around the time you and I were talking six years ago. I was frustrated with the tradition of men being in charge in the Catholic Church. That just continued to bristle against me for some reason. I think I started finding community and peace and encouragement elsewhere. When I was in college and certainly when I was growing up as a member of a really Catholic family, the local church was my community; it was my social life; it was my worldview, and it also made up my understanding of what spirituality was. When I left college I pretty much stopped going to Mass. It was a bit of frustration with the women's priest thing, and it was also a change in my own lifestyle. When I would go to Mass I would increasingly be frustrated—I don't know if I can put my finger on exactly why. Francis hasn't changed the Church's stance toward marriage equality; he hasn't changed the stance toward allowing women into the priesthood—it just doesn't seem he can do that much. On the women's issue, for me it is too late."

Now **Rachael**. "I am still waiting for Francis to do a little more on the women's issue. I don't know whether I am called to be ordained or not. I don't know that answer, but I do know that I am being asked to step into roles that are sacramental with a small *s*. This is especially true with my ministry in the prison— such as offering blessings. I will preach; I helped plan the Good Friday liturgy and the Passion narrative, and am helping with the bilingual aspects of the Mass for Hispanic women in prison. When I am ministering in the prison there is no question that the inmates believe I am capable. I provide support and accompany them, and they do this to me. Where do I think Pope Francis is on the ordination of women? I don't know. I feel good that the commission on the women diaconate is happening, and it was a savvy thing for him to call it into being. My hunch is that he may defer and leave it up to local bishops to decide whether women could be ordained to the diaconate. But I don't think that is enough. I think we need a renewal of the priesthood and what that means. I can say I am not called to be ordained into the priesthood system as it currently is. I am not interested in the diocesan priesthood, which is very isolating. My hunch is that he 'gets' that there needs to be change, but he is also of a different generation so it is hard to know what he might do. There are plenty of men in formation for the priesthood who do not think that women should be ordained, as well as plenty of them who do—it's a mixed bag. I myself did not think of it as a justice issue until the last six months because I didn't think about this as shaping our moral imagination and what we see in Church. This is new for me. I continue to think and pray over this. If I see a woman up on the altar, such as for a communion service, that changes things, and it is really sacred; it is sacramental."

The final reflection comes from **Paul**, who, although realizing the pope had to uphold Pope John Paul II's mandate not even to discuss this issue, sees some hope in the way Francis made his declaration. "Regarding his dealings with women in the Church, I look at it in two ways. I am disappointed that he stated, regarding women's ordination, that this is settled doctrine. Francis seems to have put the final coat of paint on that, and that is the way it is going to be. And yet, I don't know the way Francis stated it, but he seemed to have affirmed this doctrine in such a way as there was still a glimmer of hope in it. I saw a glint in his eye, as if saying, 'Well it's settled but. . . .' I am influenced by something I read on adaptive leadership. One of the elements of this theory is that you have to gradually ripen issues for people. You have to prepare people for radical changes by slowly shining light on the fruit until it ripens. In that regard, I think he is creating the situation where some change can come about, but it won't come about in his pontificate, at least I don't think so. The Church is still really fighting against the nineteenth century and modernist tendencies. Most people are kind of beyond that. He is gradually ripening these areas, such as married men becoming priests. He has to lay the paving stones one at a time. We are in Oz at this time, paving the Yellow Brick Road. I think we just have to hang in there and hope for the best."

Reactions to the Ordination of Women

The responses from both those who have moved on and those who have remained regarding the ordination of women touched upon these issues:

- Those who are no longer Catholic are not as passionate about this as are those who are still members. The limitations placed on women in the Church may have been one of the reasons for leaving, but now they are settled into a new way of worshiping and praying, and have found another community with whom to identify. They still want the Church to change its stance on ordaining women, but if that happened, most of them would not return to the Catholic Church again.

- The role of women in the Church includes having a part to play in the decision making and leadership of the Church. It also includes the possibility of being ordained to the priesthood. While not happening at the present moment, this issue still needs to get out into the open and be the subject of conversation and dialogue. It deserves careful discussion and guided debate among all of the faithful, not just among the hierarchy. It can no longer be swept under the rug and left untouched.

- Attitudes among those who continue to call themselves Catholic differed on the subject of women's ordination. The people's responses lay along a continuum that stretched from those who believe that ordaining women would not be a good idea—a minority position—to those who want to see a change made in the very near future. This was also a minority position.

- The feelings of most of the Catholics interviewed fell somewhere in between the two extremes. "Yes," they say, "it has to happen, but we need to go slowly." "Let the fruit ripen," as **Paul** suggested or as **Jane** cautioned, "He has to go at a slower pace because he would get too much pushback from the Curia and conservative members of the faithful if he made sudden changes."

- Many of those who are remaining in the Church felt that having women deacons was a good start toward including women. It might, they suggested, get the ball rolling toward the eventual ordination of women to the priesthood. A few of those who had left the Church also praised Francis for forming a commission to discuss this possibility. As **Mark** mentioned, "He rightly has been praised for seeming to be a more progressive pope than Benedict was in his openness to having women deacons, which is admirable."

- Some of those interviewed, both in and out of the Church, considered the ordination of women as a matter of justice. In their minds, more than half of all Catholics are women, and they need to be treated with equal dignity and respect as full members of the Church, including access to all aspects of Church governance. The world is moving swiftly ahead in this regard, they contested, leaving the Church farther and farther behind.

- Also in terms of justice, there is the matter of the needs of the faithful not being addressed because of an acute shortage of priests in many parts of the world. Not having celibacy as a requirement for ordination could relieve the pressure as married men fill the ranks of the priesthood. But the unique gifts that women priests could offer in dealing with sensitive issues related to relationships, family matters, sexuality, and concerns of justice would help meet the needs of many more people, especially fellow women like themselves.

- As mentioned a number of times by those interviewed, the work of the Holy Spirit was evident in the election of Pope Francis. The Spirit, according to people's accounts, also seems to be drawing some women toward the special call of priesthood. This vocation, in other words, does not belong solely to men. **Rachael** wondered if she had this call. "I don't know whether I am called to be ordained or not. I don't know that answer, but I do know that I am being asked to step into roles that are sacramental with a small *s*."

- Has Francis made a difference? Yes, he definitely has, by providing a climate of openness in which many new topics can be brought forward. Forming a commission to study the question of women becoming deacons has stimulated much discussion on both sides, for and against. People are experiencing a new freedom to voice their opinions, which is something they have not felt before. As previously mentioned, **Paul** thought he noticed something subtle in Francis's demeanor. "I don't know the way Francis stated it, but he seemed to affirm this doctrine in such a way as there was still a glimmer of hope in it. I saw a glint in his eye, as if saying, 'Well it's settled but . . .'"

Chapter 13

The Parish Response

Chapter 4 included a list of suggestions for improving parish life and operations. It came from those who had left the Catholic Church before Francis was elected pope. Their checklist included the following:

- Accepting people as they are and listening to their concerns
- Making the liturgies more engaging and relevant to people's lives
- Fostering an inclusive community that is open to all comers
- Dealing openly with social justice issues
- Reaching out to those in need or in trouble

The Pastor Sets the Tone

Not many of the former Catholics who were interviewed had much to say about the effect that Francis's pontificate had on the local parish. Only five out of twenty-one people made a comment about their previous experience of parish life. **Peggy** was one of them. "Priests have to be open to the people," she said, "and not think that they are better than the people. They have to remember that they are there to help the people and to guide." She then added this remark: "I have run into some priests who were just nasty. I think the quality of the priests has to improve. I have no idea how to go about that. My friends who still go to Catholic churches are saddened by the quality of the priests. The younger priests don't seem to have joy. They are very 'cut and dry.' They seem to be more deaf to the needs of the people than the old guys."

In **Mary Jo**'s opinion, not much has changed in the parish since Francis became pope. According to her, "The weird thing is that it has gotten worse." She recounted a poor experience she had with a priest who, although in town, chose not to have any role in the funeral or last rites of her mother. The associate pastor was not much better. "The whole funeral from a Church perspective certainly wasn't pastoral. For me it reinforced all of the reasons why I left the Church. The associate pastor who was the presider was horrible. His homily was not personal in any shape or form. For me, the worst part was that, unlike my father's funeral where the children brought up objects representing his work and livelihood, when we asked to do the same for my mother's funeral, the priest said that this was not allowed anymore. It is no longer part of the liturgical standards. I don't need any of those little things in my life." She acknowledged that this may not be typical, and, as she put it, "Some parishes do it well." She continued by saying, "To be fair to them, we are expecting pastors to do more with less. That is a challenging work environment for them to be in."

For **Jamie**, there are many churches of different faiths in her area that are collaborating efforts to serve the larger community and are dialoguing with one another. "The pope is doing this with different faiths as well," she pointed out. "This makes me happy." But then she added, "The local Catholic parish does not seem to be as active in these dialogues and shared efforts."

Andrew felt training was the key. "Francis's approach has to get down to the parish level, and this can't happen without training. There needs to be an organized training and development process for current pastors to help them make the transition from a top-down approach to participative leadership. The pastors will need to be coached to make this change. This will have to be done on the diocesan level—a formal process for training and coaching pastors. Unfortunately, the pastors are overworked and don't have the time to change the system and try out a new way of acting. Francis is pulling the hierarchy, kicking and screaming, in this direction. It is a big challenge, but this is what it would take. This is how Francis operates—as a Servant Leader."

The Local Parish

In contrast to the few former Catholics who commented on the local scene, two-thirds of those who chose to remain in the Church offered insights. Unlike the direct impact Francis had on these people's personal lives, many said that Francis had little or no affect on the parish they attended or on the diocese as a whole. **Kristy** confessed, "I have not seen any change in our archdiocese. They are still doing the same old stuff. The pope's charism of helping the poor is not being played out in this archdiocese. The archbishop is not championing the homeless cause here. But he is still building a large home for himself. There is not much in the archdiocesan newspaper. What Francis is saying should be exploding onto the pages of this paper. It is not. Only a few parishes seem to be changing in their outreach to the homeless and in social justice issues. It all depends on who is the pastor and not necessarily because of Francis."

Following a change of pastors, **Barbara** found her parish moving backward rather than forward. "There is absolutely no evidence of any influence of Francis on our local parish, none. In fact, I think the priests at our parish think Francis is a heretic; I really do. Since we first talked in 2011, at least half of our parishioners have disappeared. Members of our parish would meet in private homes to discuss what our options were after the new priests came in. Early on, when we were struggling with the priests that were sent to run our parish, I said to the group of parishioners, 'This is good for us. I am studying more now, and reading more. It is like a wakeup call for us.' Before this, we were complacent and happy in our Vatican II–spirit parish; it didn't prompt me to study and read as much as I did when there was a change of pastors. I am thankful for that, to learn from negative experiences."

Anne lamented the parishes that were losing membership. "Some parishes are empty, and pastors have nothing to do. This is sad. Many priests were trained before Francis. They are part of a Church that is made up of rules. For them there should be no extras in the way the liturgy is celebrated. Where are we going with Francis as our pope?" Her answer centered on his appointment of new bishops who are willing to move ahead in the direction he is suggesting through his writings and personal witness. **Danielle** saw evidence of this taking place when her own pastor was made a bishop. "It makes us sick to have lost him—it was like losing a family member. We were grieving because that is what we want in a parish priest, not just want but what we *need* in a parish priest. He challenged us, over and over. When you look at the excellent appointments that have been made recently, it makes me excited for the whole Church."

This hopeful optimism was somewhat tempered by what **Dan** observed. "There are places and parishes where people are not impacted by Francis. They remember the good old days of Pope John Paul II and the move back to orthodoxy, resisting what is going on in the world. Francis brings to communities the idea that you had better be in the world. If you are going to be a pastor, he wants you to smell like the sheep—you better get into the thick of it. This translates to the lay people as well. Francis is making a difference to parish vitality in places that are open to it. Some parishes do have an understanding of the Gospel and mission that is 'in the street.' It is just like breathing to them. I think Francis makes a difference in parishes like that, and people like that, and pastors like that. They are very buoyed up by it."

That is not, however, what everyone experienced in their local parish. In response to the question, "Does Francis make a difference on the local level?" **Claudia** responded, "He does and he doesn't. In the long run, it is the parish priests who don't all like what he is saying. He is upsetting the apple cart. It really depends on what parish you are in and who the pastor is and how he delivers Francis's message. There are those priests who very much support the Francis doctrine—helping the poor, helping those in need, following his priorities. The pastor sets the tone and models it through his behavior and lifestyle."

Maureen agreed. When asked whether the parish was different after Francis became pope, she remarked, "Pastor, pastor, pastor is the important part of the parish." She admitted that her own parish had not changed and felt that most other parishes had not been affected much either, with a few exceptions. "I would say that the local church has not been impacted very much by the pope. That is not so in all cases. We all know certain parishes that have dynamic pastors and staffs who can impact people's lives in a positive way, including their hearts and their souls. Francis has made a difference in these parishes. They have listened to him and paid attention; they have integrated his philosophy into their parishes. But I no longer look to my parish to feed me. I go to church because of the community of the people, and that is why I remain Catholic. I could also be of any other faith and be the same way; I just happen to be a Catholic. I feed myself in other ways, and I realize I am fortunate in that I have many ways to feed myself spiritually that other people don't have. I tell my own kids and others as well, 'It is okay to shop around and find a place that will feed you. If some place doesn't feed you, go elsewhere.' It is true, especially with young people, that they are at a loss because there is no place they can go to find a good parish. If you don't know anybody related to a parish, you don't know whom to ask. But God knows all that. We just need to trust and do our part."

Joanne also felt frustrated with the lack of priests and pastors who followed in the footsteps of Francis and tried to bring positive changes to the parish. "We worked so hard to keep the leadership structure alive in my previous parish. Where are those priests who are willing to be inclusive and collaborative? They must be out there."

Kathleen felt it didn't matter that much as long as there was community. "If I don't like the pastor, or the bishop, or even the pope, I still have the people around me to keep me firm in my Catholic faith and identity."

A change of pastors, however, did make a big difference to **Fayann,** and the affect was not pleasant. "At one time our parish was flourishing, and it was a happy place where people attended with enthusiasm. This is all gone now—the people are gone. Those who are still there are enjoying an old-time church they knew as children—it is too bad. When the new priests came in, the school closed. The parents left because they didn't like the type of religion that the new priests insisted upon teaching." This is not exactly a manifestation of a parish modeled on Pope Francis's actions and priorities.

The change of pastor was also devastating for **Caroline.** "I think some of Francis's more open ideas and welcoming haven't reached our local parish. I had to leave our local parish right after a new pastor took over about the time of our last interview. I loved our local parish up to that point. I don't keep close track of what is going on, but the pastor's ways of thinking and being are not what our Pope Francis is all about—and that makes me stay away from that parish." She went on to lament, "Even though Pope Francis is a fantastic person and has all of these wonderful beliefs and openness, why is this not happening on the local level? There must be a better way. This is a disappointment to me and is proof that the Catholic Church is not working so well and needs to change."

Larry also voiced frustration with the limited extent to which the pope's lifestyle and personal example have been realized in the parish. "In listening to his message and seeing him living with poor people, his understanding the poor and having more open borders regarding the Church, I don't think that gets translated well into a lot of parishes. I am saddened by that, because I think the Church in this country could be and should be a more powerful force in what goes on in the political arena. To be fair, I have heard priests say from the pulpit, 'Francis has said this or that,' and they have said it in a positive way such that we, the people, should listen more carefully to the pope."

For **Lucy**, it has been business as usual in her parish. "Not much has changed in the liturgy because of Pope Francis. His appointments seem very hopeful, but it hasn't filtered down to the parish level yet." **Terry** felt the same way. "Our own parish is pretty neutral about Francis—there are no anti-abortion talks, but no pro-immigration talks either." A similar sentiment was mentioned by **Pam**. "Francis's influence on the parish? Nothing I can think of in particular. I know our pastor has made reference to him before, but I can't think of an example. I don't feel Pope Francis's presence during our parish Masses."

On a more positive note, **Phillip**, a member of a parish staff, felt his parish was doing a great job in following the pope's example and teachings. "The priests' preaching does include Francis and his working with the poor. This is an affirmation of what he has been doing. The grace, though, is that when something like *Laudato Si'* comes out, and we want to be able to share this with the community at large, I have always had free rein to do that. We did a book discussion on *Laudato Si'* here, and it was the largest participation we ever had. I think the environment issue really hit people right between the eyes, and they wanted to share their opinions on that. The next Francis writing we are going to take on with the parish is *Amoris Laetitia*, especially with marriage ministry—we need to change how we look at folks."

For **Ginny**, "The fact that Francis is with the people is what makes a difference. That can happen with us. If he were here, he would not be removed from us. He would be with us." In other words, if Francis were the pastor of a local parish, he would be one with the people, caring for their needs but also drawing them out into the streets to look around for others who were hurting and asking for help. As Pope Francis himself stated, "Let us pray for our parishes that they not be simply offices, but that animated by a missionary spirit, they may be places where faith is communicated and charity seen" (Parishes at the Service of the Mission, www.popesvideo.org, September 2017).

Chapter 14

Could Be a Turning Point

The election of Pope Francis was a shift in the leadership of the Church. The summer of 2018 was more than a shift, it was a shaking of the foundations. In July, the prominent and popular American Cardinal, Theodore McCarrick, was forced to resign because of allegations of sexual abuse. In August, a grand-jury report was released by the attorney general of Pennsylvania that chronicled seventy years of sexual abuse by clerics and a systematic cover-up by bishops in six dioceses. The widespread response of anger, sadness, and disgust was immediate. This led to a letter by Pope Francis, dated August 20, 2018, addressed "To the People of God" throughout the world. In it he wrote, "Looking back to the past, no effort to beg pardon and to seek to repair the harm done will be sufficient. Looking ahead to the future, no effort must be spared to create a culture able to prevent such situations from happening, but also to prevent the possibility of their being covered up and perpetuated."

A flurry of outrage against the bishops and cardinals continued, even the suggestion that the pope himself should resign. On September 12, the pope announced that a gathering of the heads of all of the bishops national conferences from around the world would take place in Rome on February 21–24, 2019, to discuss the sexual abuse issue.

Although this book was in the preparation stages for being published, this critical moment in the life of the Catholic Church was too important not to be included. This could prove to be *the* moment when asking the question, "*Can Francis Change the Church?*" receives a hint of an answer from those interviewed for this book. As a result, those who told their stories and shared their wisdom in both 2012–13 and 2017 were once again contacted and asked these four questions:

1. What is your own reaction to the current situation regarding clergy abuse and the bishops' actions?
2. Has it changed or affected your own attitude and/or practice regarding the Catholic Church?
3. What changes are necessary in the Church, structurally or otherwise?
4. What do you think Pope Francis could or should do right now in light of these recent events?

Of the fifty-two who participated in the 2017 interviews, forty-five (87%) responded in the short time that was available. Sixteen were those who had left the Church and twenty-nine who had remained in the Church. What follows are their reactions, divided into the two groups of former and current Catholics.

Reactions to the Abuse Issue

The general feelings from those who no longer call themselves Catholic could be summed up in the words of **Mary Jo**, "Appalled but not surprised!" and **Christina**, "I was heartbroken, discouraged, and angry." The people may be at a distance from the Church, but their responses were, nevertheless, strong and emphatic. **Andrew** wrote, "It is an unfortunate continuation of the uncovering of what is now an obvious pattern of abuse that was known and accepted among the powerful levels of the clergy in the Catholic Church for decades, if not longer. As **Bob** put it, "I have watched the institution of the Church move further and further from the mission of Jesus."

Sadness was the predominant emotion felt by **Connie**. "I felt and still feel sadness. Sadness for those who have had a lifetime of hiding and being ignored for what happened to them. Sadness for the Church that it feels so other than human, that it had to hide shame and embarrassment for what happens within. All of this goes against everything that is taught."

Mike's reaction was different now than it was in the past. "I didn't have the same reaction as I did back in 2002, the first time the sex abuse had erupted. I think it is because I am no longer a member of the Catholic Church. I felt a little more resigned and distant from it now than before. It didn't disrupt me as much. I was very disappointed but not particularly surprised, I guess. When I talked to family members and others who are still active Roman Catholics, their sense of it was "not again." They wondered when will it ever end. I kind of wondered about that, too."

Theresa found most fault with the bishops. "The priests may have a problem which needs addressing because they cannot control it. But the bishops, of all people in this world, should be standing up to do the right thing even when it is so hard. Not sure we knew thirty years ago what we know now about pedophiles—that cures are very rare and additional controls need to be in place. But I also think most bishops took the easy way out—not rocking the boat, especially for these poor priests they cared about so much."

Strong sentiments also came from those who still consider themselves Catholic. For Pam it was being sad and losing trust. "My own reaction to clergy abuse is that of disgust and sadness. I feel sad for the victims and angry on their behalf. I feel sad for Catholics, that this is what our Church is known for. I feel sad for the clergy who are innocent to these charges and abuses. I feel sad for the leaders of the Church that they have to defend themselves and our Church. But mostly, I feel distrust. I don't know whom to trust in the Catholic Church anymore." Loss of trust was the issue for Caroline as well. "I think it's disgusting and makes me sick to my stomach, doubly so because these are the 'holy' men who are supposed to lead us to deepen our spirituality. How could we ever possibly trust that they could do that when so many are raping and molesting our children and/or adults?"

Besides disgust, there was a sensitivity among the respondents as well. **Jane** remarked, "I think my reaction to everything is really sadness. It casts a pall over the good-hearted, nonoffending priests who are true to their ministry and not involved in this scandal." **Ed** added, "We are a Church made up of human beings, with warts, wrinkles, and lovely wonders." But that was not what came from **Danielle**. "There is much anger in my heart, mind, and gut at those bishops who put their own sanctimonious ego ahead of what was right for the victims. Not one of them cared about the victims, only about hiding themselves and the abusers from the public eye. From 1983, and from 2002, and again now, the phrase they liked to use was, 'I thought I was saving Mother Church from scandal.' Not then, not now, not ever has that been true! What did Jesus have to say about harming one of these little ones? Sounds appropriate to me today."

Clericalism was the issue for **Joanne**. "I'm sickened by the clericalism that is so pervasive. My children are asking me why I don't feel embarrassed to stay Catholic, and I'm having a difficult time coming up with a satisfactory answer. I know the Church is not the hierarchy, and I want to believe that with every fiber of my being. But the fact is, the hierarchy is a VERY, VERY LARGE part of this Church. Increasingly, the hierarchical aspect of the Church as an institution feels like it's suffocating the faithful people who are coming to Mass each week for spiritual food."

The sentiments of both past and current members of the Church can be summed up with the feelings of **Allyson**. "What can I say really? I'm angry. I'm embarrassed. I'm hurt. In many ways it all feels surreal. How can the Church, the Church that I trusted and have had as a center for my whole life, have done something like this—be the source of such pain? It's hard to wrap my head around it honestly. It has made me reevaluate why I believe what I believe and why I choose to be Catholic. I'm not going to leave the Church, but I, in no way, condone the actions of the abusive clergy nor those who covered their actions."

People's Attitudes and Practices

For those who had left the Church, there was not much of a change in their actions. They remain at a distance, feeling sadness for the Church they once loved. They continue to worship, pray, and identify with a community elsewhere.

Most of the comments were similar to what **Mike** expressed: "In the past I wondered whether I should return to the Catholic Church, but when things like this happen, it validates my decision to leave. A lot of it has to do with the reactions of some bishops that the Church needs to be defended at all costs. Even when priests do these horrible things, the Church's reputation must be retained. Church authority takes precedence over a pastoral response or asking forgiveness. The mindset is to protect the institution. As long as the Church stays in that mode, it's not going to improve. How much is it going to take to bring the clericalism to the ground? There are so many good things that stand to be destroyed. The danger is that the good will be lost with the bad."

Sally, who at one time was thinking of joining the Catholic Church, has now gone in the opposite direction, "I chose not to become a Catholic a while back, but had been willing to go with my husband occasionally. At this time both my husband and I would not consider attending a Catholic Church unless there was a total reorganization. Every priest, bishop, or cardinal who had any part in the offenses or cover-ups should be removed. My husband, who was raised Catholic, says he won't say never, but he would only consider giving the Church a chance if it became more modern and after 'cleaning house' of the current perpetrators. He says he will not give a penny to the Church and will be disgusted if money is used to give these priests legal services and luxury homes."

A change of direction also happened in **Peggy's** life as a result of current revelations. "Yes, it has changed my attitudes because I was actually thinking about going back to church again. My attitude that was growing positive has now gone back to being negative. I used to speak to people about their relationship with God that was not dependent upon the priest in front of them. Now I feel differently. The priest is important—but now for me not in a positive way."

For many of those who have left, the comments made by **Mary Jo** reflected their own attitudes, "It has reinforced my distrust of the institution and its intentions, and has strengthened my resolve to distance myself from the Church."

Regarding the religious practices of those who have remained Catholic, three out of twenty-nine either have made the choice to leave the Church or are close to it. This amounts to 10 percent of the total. **Tom** remarked, "Yes, I give up." **Phillip** responded, "I'm keeping my distance now." **Caroline** commented, "Right now I am choosing to attend a United Church of Christ service where all are truly welcomed and, hopefully, not abused."

For the others, although they still practice their Catholic faith, their attitudes have shifted, especially with regard to the hierarchy. **Richard** expressed it this way: "It has not changed my going to Mass. That's my community. My idea about the Church has changed in that I used to trust the bishops but I don't any more." **Allyson** felt the same way. "The short answer is yes, my attitudes have changed, but not in a way that drives me from the Church. For me, these scandals have reinforced the fact that members of the clergy are human and therefore fallible. I don't follow them, I follow Christ. I believe that we were all given a conscience, a sense of right and wrong, to interpret the world the best we can and to follow him. He is the true teacher and guide. He is my Lord. While I will continue to follow and trust the priest of my parish, I will keep in mind that he is still human."

Jane separated the institutional Church from her own spiritual life by stating, "I keep the distinction between the formal institution of the Church and the personal spiritual message of Jesus Christ. The latter stands at the center for me. The institution, on the other hand, is a vehicle, whose wheels are off the tracks right now." The same was true for **Maureen**, "We cannot let the structure of the Church and our relationship with God be merged. They are two separate things. That is why I think my attitude or practices have not been changed, nor will they, by the abuse issue. The two are two totally separate entities. Over the years, if I didn't want to lose my faith, I just had to keep the two separate." **Anne** put it more succinctly: "I'm not going to let the misbehaviors of the bishops affect my own faith."

Changes in the Church

Those interviewed were asked, "What changes are necessary in the Church, structurally or otherwise?" A few radical responses came from those who no longer called themselves Catholic. One was what **Mary Jo** had to offer. "Fire all current leaders and replace them with lay people who have the expertise and experience to lead as Jesus would have." **Jack** added, "It's definitely time for the Church to allow married and female clergy." **Sally** agreed, "Allow priests to be married. Allow women to serve. Stop the 'boys club' and stop treating the higher-ups like such royalty." **Christina** felt the same way. "The pattern of abuse and cover up in the Church has proven to be pervasive and expansive, reaching the highest levels of leadership. Nothing short of a complete overhaul and restructuring is needed."

Others focused more on the immediate issue of covering up those who caused the abuse. As **Peggy** said, "First of all, I think that anytime a child is sexually abused, it has to be reported to the police. Those in charge don't even talk to the person accused. Let the police deal with the crime that was committed. But the Church has to deal with this as well. Under previous popes, these pedophile priests were just moved around. Someone must hold the bishops and hierarchy accountable, people other than themselves because they are not trustworthy. The change must be within the structure itself—how bishops are selected and what their job is. Right now the bishops are so far removed from the people on an everyday or every Sunday basis; they are not there. The bishops cannot sit there like little royalties, because that is how they are treated. They become royalty."

Andrew called for a new of way of considering sexual abuse. In his words, "The clergy abuse issue is just as heinous as rape and murder." He went on to say, "There is an obvious need for a completely new mindset and belief system of what are appropriate and acceptable relationships. There must be a willingness to come forward with full disclosure and swift action to deal with the offenders. Structurally, there will need to be nonclergy on the review and oversight committees. Not allowing this is akin to having fraternities or police departments be self-regulated. It is too difficult to see and accept peers (often friends) objectively because most offenders are masters at keeping this personality and sexual disorder hidden."

Mike felt the problem begins before ordination, when future priests go through formation. "There is a need to rethink the priesthood in the Church, more as being a shepherd. My impression is that those coming out of the seminary are climbing back up on the pedestal. They want to be seen in that role. Priestly formation needs to have more to do with humility and the servant model of priesthood. The idea that the priest is the head of the parish and that 'Father' knows best is not appropriate. Father does not know best, and hopefully the people will be wiser, smarter, and holier than Father, especially when Father is only twenty-eight years old."

There were many more suggestions for changes in the Church coming from those who are still Catholic than from those who had left. Those who remain have more to say because it affects them more directly. The responses are grouped under three headings: the involvement of the laity, the role of women, and the requirements for ordination.

The Laity

A number of those interviewed called for the laity to take a more active role in the various structures and decision-making process of the Church, bottom to top. **Ed**, while appreciating the size of the shift, called for a complete change in Church governance. "The task is enormous, the resistance is palpable and seemingly impossible. A deep conversion is essential. Is it time to convene a Vatican Council III, but this time with deliberative decision-making power by the whole Church, the People of God?" **Anne** suggested an oversight committee, or as she called it, "an independent inquiry board comprised entirely of lay people. It needs to look into the basic flaw that has exempted bishops from the sexual abuse process. It needs to answer the question of how cardinals and archbishops rose in their ecclesiastical careers when troubling facts regarding sexual abuse were known by the hierarchy that promoted them."

On the local level, **Danielle** suggested, "Calling more lay people to active participation in our parishes, churches, and dioceses. Our voices are needed if we are to grow spiritually in our discipleship. It is time to be partners with our parish priest, and if we have to, train him! It is appropriate to ask our parish priest, 'When is the next time you will make reports to the bishop? The pastoral council will go with you in solidarity!' There is transparency in this approach. There are also many diocesan commissions and committees in which people could serve. We need to educate ourselves more about the workings of our diocese so as not to be caught off guard. It is OUR Church, too!"

Joanne addressed the problem of clericalism. "The hierarchy must begin to truly share power and leadership in a meaningful way. I want to trust that the Holy Spirit is working and that God will not abandon us. The sad consequence of the lack of accountability within the hierarchy is that the Church has frittered away its moral authority. The Church has been its own worst enemy by destroying its credibility. The bishops need to bring in respected lay experts to thoroughly and transparently investigate the diocesan records related to sexual abuse and the abuse of power, then prepare reports as soon as possible. If they don't, the attorneys general will come after them, as has happened in a number of dioceses."

Along the same lines, **Rachael** proposed setting up structures of accountability for bishops. "There needs to be actual mechanisms in place for bishops to report inappropriate, illegal, and unethical behavior that they observe among other bishops in order to foster transparency and responsible behavior. This must be rooted in lay leadership. We have no shortage of people who are perfectly capable of doing this important job. Think Truth and Reconciliation Boards found in other countries."

"The necessary changes in the Church," voiced **Kathleen**, "are to bring the laity in, full force. We are a huge hunk of the Church. Our laity have done wonderful work, and we are important to the Church, but we have not been making the decisions. We need to be part of deciding what the Church is going to look like; and if there are going to be changes, it has to pass through our okay."

The Role of Women

The current crisis in the Church has heightened the remarks made in earlier chapters on women. As **Denise** mentioned, "First and foremost, women need to be included at EVERY level of the institutional Church." **Danielle** remarked, "Here is the elephant in the room. When will the institutional Church recognize the gifts of the women in our Church. Where are the feminine voices? Lay people need to find their voices in the institutional Church if they want meaningful changes. God gave us brains to use for ALL her creations. The Church is one of them."

Larry felt that much was missing because women are not given their rightful place in the Church. "Bring women into leadership positions at the highest levels even if you don't want to ordain them. So much of what is human, caring, inclusive, watchful, and loving is by and large better expressed by women, or at least better expressed by men and women together."

Maureen took the role of women to the core of the institutional structure. "There need to be women in leadership positions in the Church. It is despicable that no women are there. There must be more involvement of everyone in all aspects of the Church. Appoint a woman to be a cardinal. You don't need ordination for that. As laity, let's be leaders in the Church, not followers." Terry had the same idea, only more so. "Perhaps it would work to name women cardinals who do not need to be ordained. Have six or eight as part of the College of Cardinals. It may not be doable, but it is the sort of radical change that is needed."

Barbara took a more historical perspective, drawing on practices dating back to when the Church was in its infancy. "Is it not time then for the institutional Church to promote a truly radical reform of its structure, one that could renew its being in accordance with a spirit that historians detect in early Christianity where women as well as men shared roles of leadership and authority? Anything less than such a reform is destined to leave essentially unchanged a fetid system."

Requirements for Ordination

The issue of women's ordination was discussed in Chapter 12. This theme returned as people offered suggestions for structural changes in the Church following the sex abuse scandal. Tom thought that a more inclusive priesthood would be a good way to reach out to young adults. "Make the Church relevant to our modern times, especially for our younger generations. Married priests and woman priests would be a good start." Lucy felt the same way. "For the Church, it's time to open up the clergy to include women priests and married priests, and to drop the celibacy requirement. It's time for action, not allegations or apologies."

Caroline offered these two suggestions: (1) They should allow priests to be married and have families. This would attract healthier people into the priesthood. (2) Allow women to be ordained into the priesthood." **Kristy** made this plea: "I think there need to be women in leadership roles in the bishop's office, and in the Curia, and in most Church offices. I think women bring a unique gift, and when they are hired they need to come with power and authority. I don't believe in forming advisory committees of women who can advise the bishop or archbishop or other clergy types. I have been on too many advisory committees. Ultimately we need to ordain women and have married priests. We've got to, we do!"

Finally, these positive thoughts came from **Ginny**: "This is a good moment for the Church. There needs to be a change of basic structures because the present structures are not working. There needs to be a new way of including nonclerics, including women, in the decision making of the Church, new structures of shared decision making.

"Look at the ordination of women. What we need is partnership with men and women at every level of the hierarchical structure. I think the hierarchical structure itself needs to be looked at. Include at every level of decision making the voices of the People of God. There needs to be a place for the *sensus fidelium* (the sense of the people) to be heard and considered in decision making at all levels. The introduction of women at those levels will make a significant difference. That is not to say that women are incapable of sin. We certainly are, but I think it would make a difference. I'm not saying that women are perfect or not without their faults, but I think the complementarity of gifts is very, very important for the Church."

What Francis Should Do

Despite their withdrawal from the Church, those on the outside looking in had much to offer regarding what decisions the pope needs to make and what actions he needs to take at this time. For instance, **Nancy** said, "Pope Francis is a smart, compassionate, revered person, but to me that is what he should be instead of an exception to these qualities. I want my pope to be, at this point in time, a very bold, loud, demanding, daily voice, one who is championing changes that need to take place in the Church." Make note that while not a practicing Catholic, she still considered Francis as "my pope."

She is not alone in wanting bold action. **Mike** went so far as to ask for the resignation of all bishops. "What the pope perhaps should do is ask for the resignation of all of the bishops. Part of me thinks that would be good, but then I am also thinking what other problems might that raise. I would not want the pope to lose the good bishops that he has appointed recently. The question is how to hold the bishops accountable. I don't see any formal process for removing bishops from their diocese and appointing someone new who can be trusted. I was surprised how quickly he responded to the Church in Chile, having all of the bishops offer their resignations and accepting this from four of the bishops."

Another bold move was suggested by **Christina**. "He could invite input from Catholics all over the world on their vision for the Catholic Church and then shepherd an open and transparent process for reordering the Church. He could also actively promote the ordination of women, eliminate the vow of celibacy, and allow all ordained priests (male and female) to marry."

Peggy pleaded for something more immediate. "He has to give the bishops a dressing down. I don't think he should be nice at this point. The way Francis reacted toward the Chilean bishops was great, where they all gave in their resignations. If the bishops can't be, each and every day, just like everybody else, primarily because they are Christians, then their statements and pronouncements are just a bunch of words. When I read the letters that the bishops send out, I say to myself, 'Really?' Christianity is a grassroots religion. The hierarchy sees itself as 'above' the grassroots. This should not be. It should be people helping people. Pope Francis has done a good job with this."

Not nearly as many suggestions of what the pope should do came from those who had left as came from those who have remained in the Church. The latter want to be heard because it is "their Church," and they look to Francis to initiate the changes they deem necessary. "I like our pope very much," said **Larry**, "but he, too, must be more directive even in the face of opposition. Great words and one-liners aren't enough at this point."

These were also the suggestions **Tom** made to the pope. "Lead the way! Be strong! Be not afraid! Propose and promote *real changes*, recognizing and realizing the stiff opposition that you will encounter. Reform the culture of the Church itself, knowing that this will not happen quickly but will take years and years, even centuries. Get started now. Either that or watch the Church deteriorate and see millions of people lose their faith."

"Act now!" was also the advice voiced by **Ed**. "Maintain your apparent good humor and faith that the Holy Spirit is in charge. But act swiftly. Immediate, decisive, transparent disclosure of these matters might help stem the justifiable rage that currently baffles and infuriates the People of God."

"Don't give in!" was the message from **Kristy**. "I think Francis should stand firm. I think he should punish those who have moved the accused around to different dioceses. And there are plenty of those. At one point I thought he should call for the resignation of all bishops and archbishops in the United States and have them reapply for their position. Then I thought, that would be counterproductive. But I think he needs to really stand firm."

In gratitude, **Ginny** remarked, "Thank God we have Francis as our pope. He can shepherd us through the necessary changes. I would want him to know that I support him 100 percent. I know what a difference he has made for Catholics in the ranks. They see him as a sign of hope, freshness, and vitality. He needs to trust his intuition, to consult, and then do what he believes the Spirit is calling him to do while he has the authority he has.

This could be an incredible moment of transition in terms of reexamining the hierarchical structures of the Church, and the male-ordained-only reality that our Church is for the most part. Francis needs to radically address that question. He is going to have an extreme right-wing reaction, but he has an opportunity here for the phoenix to rise out of the ashes of this sex abuse scandal in ways that can bring the Church into the future, to revitalize it and make it more relevant. It is just so out of touch."

"Hear the lament," was the advice from **Rachael**. "Listen, listen, listen to the victims and survivors. Have the humility, grace, and courage to call a spade a spade. Francis is in a tremendous position of power. If he calls for naming what it is, the bishops will more likely follow suit. He must model what it could look like to really repent and lament. He needs to take ownership, and begin the process of healing. I think this is a crucial moment in Francis's papacy, and, more importantly, it's a crucial moment for the People of God. We have a right to know what has happened, the sins of omission and overt cover-up. We should not be the ones who have to leave! This is our beloved Church, and Jesus is our anchor."

Kathleen also focused on the victims of abuse. "First of all, I think Francis should come out strongly for the victims and against the perpetrators. The punishment has to fit the crime. The pope has to somehow gather the bishops together to carry home the message. Nobody is believing that now. There is a lack of trust in the leaders. The laity need to make the priests and bishops understand that we have a position in the Church and that we are going to exercise it."

"Include the laity," was the message from a number of those interviewed. **Anne** remarked, "I encourage Francis to put together a board made up of laity to investigate the actions of the bishops and give this board full authority to uncover the facts. Then have the pope listen to what it uncovered and act on the information, telling the bishops that they also have to respond to the findings of the lay board." **Pam** had the same idea.

"I think Pope Francis should take a bold and strong step and hire an objective lay organization to investigate the corruption in the Catholic Church."

"I support very much the pope's efforts to be collegial," offered **Ginny**, "and to include others who are beyond the hierarchical structures. I think he needs to include the laity in his consultations. I don't mean people who are far right or far left, but people who are balanced, who are rational, dependable, who can listen and give Francis different perspectives than the ordained clergy can."

"An open Church" was the vision **Joanne** held out for Pope Francis. "He needs to have the courage to open up the Church and lead a meaningful reform that will forever change the way decisions are made in this institution. Structural change is essential now. I understand that Francis has many enemies within the ranks of the bishops and cardinals and that this is a VERY complicated matter. However, it feels as if the world is watching and waiting to see if those who hold the power in this Catholic institution will have the courage to truly share it. I fervently hope Francis will surprise me."

Conclusion

Making a Difference

It is time to take stock on whether Pope Francis is making a difference, at least to a sampling of past and present Catholics, and if he does make a difference, in what ways. The initial study took place before anyone could have predicted that (1) Pope Benedict XVI would step down and make room for a new person to take his place, and (2) that Francis would be the one taking his place.

Long before the new pope came out on the Vatican balcony asking for prayers and a blessing, there was much frustration and lack of enthusiasm among many of the faithful. Knowing this, it seemed reasonable to ask people why this was the case. The first ones questioned were the once-active Catholics who had chosen to leave the Church because, as mentioned in Chapter 2, "They had lost faith in the collective voice of the hierarchy regarding issues and concerns that meant something to them personally." Those interviewed didn't expect the Church to be perfect, but they did expect some movement in the direction of their hopes and aspirations. They did not find much evidence of this movement from those making the decisions (see "Sources of Discontent" in Chapter 2, p. 22).

Each one of these former Catholics was asked to choose a topic about which they felt strongly as a way of focusing their comments. Four topics came out on top: authority, justice—including the role of women in the Church—sexuality, and spirituality.

A second group of once-active Catholics also had difficulties with the Church, but they decided to remain within the fold, coping as best they could with an institution that did not seem interested in making needed changes. Many in this second group chose the same topics as the first, including the misuse of authority in the Church. As **Kathleen** put it, "One reason I remain in the Church is that no 'misbehaving' hierarchy is going to shove me out of *my* Church. . . . My anger over this oppressive authority comes from the demands it places on the faithful, especially the poor and less educated in the faith."

In a similar vein, **Leah** remarked, "If the Church's hierarchical institution remains stuck in its own system, it is going to clash with something very real at some point, and either will adapt and change or be left behind." Little did she know how prophetic her words would become. The Holy Spirit was working behind the scenes and preparing the ground for a seismic shift in direction. All the cares and concerns, hopes and aspirations voiced by both those who had stepped out of the Church and those who had remained were about to take a leap forward.

Welcoming the Unexpected

Those interviewed after Francis became pope were ready and willing to tell their story about how they viewed this extraordinary event. This included those who no longer called themselves Catholic, as well as those who did. They were proud to be associated with this new pope through their Catholic heritage. They no longer felt a need to hide that fact; they could hold up their heads and acknowledge their past or present Catholicity. This single change of attitude revealed that Francis had made a difference in these people's lives. "Francis is a breath of fresh air" (**Bob**). "He would be welcome around our dining room table" (**Jamie**). "I was happy that he was very humble" (**Colleen**). "I am really excited that he is the pope because he is so open-minded" (**Connie**). All of these positive comments came from people who had given up on the Church. Although no longer part of the faithful, they were praising its new leader. Those who remained Catholic were even more enthusiastic. "My anger toward the Church," **Anne** mentioned, "has mellowed because of Pope Francis." **Kathleen** was amazed at how many risks he takes and that he seems so fearless. "He is not afraid of dying, as if he were saying, 'What have I got to lose?'"

Once the initial shock and delight of the pope's election had worn off, those interviewed sensed a new direction in the Church, one that was not centered on rules and regulations so much as on a pastoral response to help those with concrete, immediate needs. According to **Richard**, "He has created a good image for the Catholic Church." Those interviewed were impressed by how the pope cut through the institutional bureaucracy and dealt with each individual he encountered with care, tenderness, and, in some cases, assistance. As **Jane** noted, "Francis put in the laundromat for the homeless in the Vatican." "Francis is giving me hope," **Kristy** remarked. "I love the way he does things. It goes back to the way Jesus would do things."

Because of the internet and social media, word about Pope Francis and what he is saying and doing gets around to people in a hurry. "The nice thing about technology and the internet," **Peggy** commented, "is that people hear what Francis actually says, and they can interpret it because they heard it directly." **Sally** added, "People are listening—they are following his tweets—it is good that they are getting his messages." Francis is making a difference by making his message simple and easy to understand. He finds the means to communicate his message and priorities directly to the faithful and to the world at large. There is no need for any intervening hierarchy or bureaucracy to spread the word; it's "out there."

As people connect with Francis, they are being challenged to change their own lives as they encounter his words and witness his example. This is true both for those who have stepped out of the Church and those who remain faithful. For each group it is making an impact on their personal lives. The awareness of the poor and marginalized has become more visible as Francis reaches out to these people wherever he travels.

A new sense of urgency to address the demands of a changing environment has also entered people's minds and hearts, and has changed behaviors. **Barbara** exclaimed, "There are so many things about him that are so good; his awareness of climate change and the horrible damage done to the environment and the need to work at changing it." "He has given us a new vision," said **Maureen**.

Pope Francis has also acknowledged the messiness of life in his comments and writings, such as *The Joy of Love (Amoris Laetitia)*; that has helped people become more understanding and less judgmental.

Fayann noticed a change in her life because of Francis. "He is engaged in the world, and that challenges me to continue to be engaged in the world as well. He is a positive influence and not a judger. How am I different now? I feel that there is an openness with Pope Francis that creates the possibility for surprises." **Anne** brings this down to the practical level. "This is where the pope affects my life now—his good decisions. What is needed is saying something nice to people. This makes such a difference. Remember to do it each day—bring this to daily prayer. Follow the example of the pope in taking the bus. Walk the streets!"

Although the pope is having an affect on people's personal lives through the news and social media, it is not being communicated through the diocese and the local parish, at least according to the experience of those who were interviewed. **Kristy**, for instance, has seen little coming through diocesan channels. "There is not much in the archdiocesan newspaper. What Francis is saying should be exploding onto the pages of this paper. It is not."

As for the parish, people complained about not hearing more about the pope from the pulpit or in parish publications. "Even though Pope Francis is a fantastic person and has all of these wonderful beliefs and openness," said **Caroline**, "why is this not happening on the local level?" **Larry** voiced a similar frustration: "In listening to his message and seeing him living with poor people, . . . I don't think that gets translated well into a lot of parishes." The impression one gets is that some bishops and pastors are not entirely on board with the new directions taken by the pope. They seem to be waiting him out. As **Claudia** put it, "In the long run, it is the parish priests who don't all like what he is saying. He is upsetting the apple cart."

The pope has been strong in confronting the hierarchy regarding those seeking positions of privilege and fostering a culture of clericalism. **Joanne** affirmed his efforts: "I hope the pope can appoint good men as bishops and cardinals, ones who see the reality of the situation and are not taken up with the trappings of their office. That is what is so important." **Kathleen** felt he was up to the job, "This pope is very politically savvy. He just is not afraid of the hierarchy. I think Francis sees people as equals."

Based on the pushback from some of the hierarchy, the question is, "Will the momentum and direction begun by Francis continue once he is no longer the pope?" No one but the Holy Spirit knows the answer. Much depends on whether there is a critical mass of cardinals who are in line with the pope's priorities by the time his pontificate has come to an end. **Mary Jo** was desirous that this would happen. "I hope Francis can live long enough to swing the pendulum a little further." **Rachael** felt that a higher power was at work in pushing that pendulum: "Will his direction continue when he is gone? I don't know, but the Spirit is moving, and the Spirit cannot be held back."

Although the response toward Pope Francis from all of those interviewed was very positive, a number of people felt he could do more to confront the sexual abuse issue that exploded in the summer of 2018, especially by including the laity more in the decision making and improving the role of women in the Church. **Mary Jo**, a person who no longer calls herself Catholic, stated, "I firmly believe God does not intend that the leadership of the Catholic Church be all male." **Barbara**, a woman who has remained Catholic, thought the pope should write an encyclical on the ordination of women akin to his treatise on climate change. "It would be truly revolutionary if the pope were to write something along the line of equality that would have a similar impact as *Laudato Si'* is having."

Others would not rule out the possibility that Francis might change his mind. **Joanne** focused on the role of the Holy Spirit regarding the ordination of women, "I have to be hopeful and believe that the Spirit is still working in the Church. If I believe that, then God will not abandon the people. We have that promise, and we have to hang on to that." **Tony**, encouraged by the pope's new emphasis, had this to say, "Francis has opened himself to seeing new things. Who knows whether he will see the women's thing differently. It may not be his priority right now, but it may become so later."

Of all the ways Pope Francis is making strides to change the Church, has he influenced those who have left the Church to return? Not significantly. Before the summer of 2018, only a few former Catholics were thinking of returning. Two people mentioned searching in earnest for a Catholic parish that might become their new faith community. This, however, changed when the revelations regarding the bishops' cover-up of sexual abuse surfaced. All of the rest have found a spiritual home for themselves somewhere else and are staying put (see "From Those Who Have Left" in Chapter 10, p. 85).

Among those who remained Catholic, a few of them are now at a greater distance from the Church. **Leah**, a young adult in her twenties, remarked, "Francis has not made a huge impact on me regarding the Church over the last four years or so. Pope Francis has not been entirely out of my scope but he has been far off the radar." **Claudia** also has been discerning her affiliation, "I feel I am at a crossroad now. I am very prayerful about what God wants me to do next. I feel like another journey is just about to begin for me."

It is true that in many ways the pope has made a difference in people's lives. There has not been, however, much change in their religious affiliation. Most of those who had left the Catholic

Church before Francis's election have remained where they are, while those who decided to stay Catholic are still present, with only two or three exceptions. Wherever their faith journey has taken them, they are pleased with the person who is the servant leader of the Church, hoping and praying that the new direction he has initiated will continue.

Francis Making a Difference

These are the aspects of Francis's pontificate that were mentioned by those interviewed four years after he was elected pope:

- A positive experience of Francis becoming pope—liking the refreshing, new image he has created
- The challenge to follow the example of the pope in their own lives and shifts in their personal priorities
- Paying attention to the needs of the poor, the needy, those on the margins and the lonely, as Francis has done
- Being impressed and moved by the pope's pastoral touch and sensitivities, his care for and attention to the individual
- The way in which the pope is in tune with the Gospels and makes Jesus present in the modern world by calling for a change of heart
- The pope's care for the world's environment through his encyclical *Laudato Si'*, and calling others to follow his lead
- Making people aware of the presence of the poor all around them and calling everyone to go to them, to get out on the streets
- Being sensitive to the messiness of life and not making judgments about "irregular" situations that people face
- Using technology, news sources, and social media to spread the word about God and Jesus in the world at large
- Francis's freedom and willingness to take risks in challenging the institution, hierarchy, and Curia to become servant leaders and not get caught up in privilege and clericalism

- His attempts to keep this new direction of the Church proceeding forward, especially with the appointment of new cardinals and bishops
- Openness to include women and those of various orientations in the life of the Church, with the hope that more opportunities for equality will be forthcoming
- People feeling comfortable discussing important issues in the Church, such as a greater role for the laity and ordination of women to the diaconate and priesthood
- Feeling proud to be associated with being Catholic and having this pope as the Church's leader, even amid issues related to sexual abuse
- An emphasis on prayer for the pope, asking God to keep him safe and healthy so he can remain pope for as long a period as possible
- A realization that the Holy Spirit is active in the Catholic Church and calls all human beings into a unity of faith, justice, mercy, forgiveness, and love

The Heart of Francis

The final words come from the pope himself. In November of 2013 he published *Evangelii Gaudium* (*The Joy of the Gospel*). It contained a description of his purpose in life, his role as pope. He called to the rest of us to follow his lead and do the same.

> *My mission of being in the heart of the people is not just a part of my life or badge I can take off; it is not an "extra" or just another moment in life. Instead, it is something I cannot uproot from my being without destroying my very self. I am a mission on this earth; that is the reason why I am here in this world. We have to regard ourselves as sealed, even branded, by this mission of bringing light, blessing, enlivening, raising up, healing, and freeing. All around us we begin to see*

nurses with soul, teachers with soul, politicians with soul, people who have chosen deep down to be with others and for others (no. 273).

Appendix

Methodology and Sampling

The Sampling

The original purpose of this book in 2010 was to discover the feelings and motivations of those who were pulling back from active involvement in the Church and parish life. Between May of 2011 and September of 2012, I interviewed fifty-five persons as a way of offering a small sampling of what people were feeling about the Catholic Church, both the larger institution and the local parish.

Because of my involvement with Catholic parishes and groups throughout the United States for forty years as founder and director of the Parish Evaluation Project (PEP), I was able to draw on a wealth of contacts to construct a list of those to be interviewed. They ranged in age from twenty to over eighty. They were spread across the country, from Maryland to California, and represented a sampling of both men and women. The criteria for being interviewed was that they had been actively involved in parish life but now were struggling with one or other aspect of the larger Church or local parish that caused them to be less committed.

Two groups were identified: one that included people who indicated that they had decided to withdraw from membership in the Church, and the other that represented those who declared themselves to still be Catholic, whatever their level of involvement might be. Listed below are the individuals contained in these two groups, first those who had left the Church when the first interviews took place in 2011–2012, followed by those who remained. The location of these people covered fifteen states, California, Colorado, Connecticut, Illinois, Indiana, Massachusetts, Maryland, Michigan, Minnesota, New Mexico, Pennsylvania, South Dakota, South Carolina, Virginia, Wisconsin, and the District of Columbia.

Those Who Had Left the Catholic Church

	Name	Gender	Age Spread (in 2011–12)
1.	Andrew	Male	50–65
2.	Arthur*	Male	65+
3.	Bob	Male	65+
4.	Bridget	Female	35–49
5.	Charlie	Male	50–64
6	Christina	Female	35–49
7	Colleen	Female	50–64
8.	Connie	Female	50–64
9.	Diane	Female	50–64
10.	Fanny	Female	20–34
11.	Jack	Male	65+
12.	Jamie	Female	35–49
13.	Jonathan	Male	20–34
14.	Mark	Male	20–34
15.	Mary Jo	Female	50–64
16.	Mike	Male	35–49
17.	Nancy	Female	65+
18.	Natalie*	Female	65+
19.	Peggy	Female	50–64
20.	Rafael	Male	20–34
21.	Sally	Female	35–49
22.	Susie	Female	50–64
23.	Theresa	Female	50–64

---

* The asterisk following a name in this and the next list indicates first interview only.

Those Who Remained In the Catholic Church

	Name	Gender	Age Spread (in 2011–12)
1.	Allyson	Female	20–34
2.	Anne	Female	65+
3.	Barbara	Female	65+
4.	Caroline	Female	50–64
5.	Claudia	Female	50–64
6.	Dan	Male	65+
7.	Danielle	Female	50–64
8.	Denise	Female	65+
9.	Ed	Male	65+
10.	Fayann	Female	65+
11.	Ginny	Female	65+
12.	Greg	Male	50–64
13.	Jane	Female	65+
14.	Joanne	Female	50–64
15.	John	Male	65+
16.	Kathleen	Female	65+
17.	Kerry	Female	35–49
18.	Kristy	Female	65+
19.	Larry	Male	65+
20.	Leah	Female	20–34
21.	Lucy	Female	50–64
22.	Maureen	Female	65+
23.	Pam	Female	35–49
24.	Paul	Male	50–64
25.	Phillip	Male	50–64
26.	Rachael	Female	20–34
27.	Richard	Male	65+
28.	Ruth*	Female	50–64
29.	Terry	Male	65+
30.	Tom	Male	65+
31.	Tony	Male	65+
32.	Wendy	Female	50–64

The Methodology

Step One. Initial contact was made by phone to describe, in general terms, the scope of the interviews and whether the person was willing to take the next step, which was a follow-up email. The email asked people to choose a topic about which they would be willing to tell their story, including authority, liturgy, women's issues, sexuality, justice, spirituality, or parish life.

Step Two. When people responded to the first email indicating their topic, they were sent a second email that contained a short, six-question survey that included the following:

1. Whether they were baptized Catholic at birth or were converts to the faith later in life.
2. To what age range did they belong: (20–34), (35–49), (50–64), (65 or older).
3. The reasons they chose the topic that they did and whether they were remaining Catholic or were moving on.
4. In a few sentences, limited to one hundred words, people were to indicate why they made the choice of remaining or moving on.
5. Finally, they were asked whether they knew of anyone else they thought should be contacted to be part of this project, along with that person's contact information.

Step Three. When people returned their answers to the survey, they were asked to write down their thoughts on the topic they had chosen as a way of getting ready for the one-on-one interview within the next two weeks, either by phone or in person. They were told that the interview would last approximately forty-five minutes to an hour. The interview would be based on three questions:

1. Why did you choose this topic to discuss?

2. Why are you remaining Catholic or choosing to move out of the Church?
3. What has led up to this decision you have made?

They were also told that all responses were anonymous and no identifying materials would be included in the results.

Step Four. After the fifty-five persons were interviewed, the results were typed up and sent to them by email for their feedback, editing, and approval. The resulting material was the basis for Part I, "The Before," of this book.

At this point, an event outside of my control happened in March of 2013 that interrupted the anticipated publication of the original manuscript: Francis was elected the new pope of the Catholic Church. Given his initial statements and unprecedented actions as the new pope, it was uncertain whether the results from the first set of interviews would remain relevant. All plans for publication came to an immediate halt. At that point it was questionable whether anything would come of this project.

Step Five. The original manuscript went into hibernation in the spring of 2013. Four years later, in January of 2017, it came back to life. I began to think that the project could be salvaged if given a new purpose and a new direction. Pope Francis continued to make a favorable impression on Catholics and to others in the world at large. The new purpose was to discover to what extent Pope Francis made a difference to those who were originally interviewed. The new working title was, *Can Francis Change the Church?: How American Catholics Are Responding to His Leadership.*

During the month of February 2017, I was able to contact fifty-three of the fifty-five originally interviewed five or six years earlier. The two remaining persons had died during the interim. These fifty-three persons were invited to participate in the second phase of the project through a follow-up interview. To my delight and amazement, all but one said they would be glad to take part in the project. From March through June of 2017, each one was interviewed and the results typed up and sent back to the people for corrections and permission to use their responses in the new book. They were also asked, during the interview, whether they would like to use their own first name for their contribution or to remain with the fictitious name used in the initial interview. Thirty-four out of fifty-two (65%) decided to use their own name, while eighteen (35%) stayed with the fictitious name that was originally given to them.

Step Six, In July and August of 2018, a new crisis faced the Church and Pope Francis. In the space of a few weeks, a prominent cardinal was removed from his position, and a grand jury in Pennsylvania released a report of sexual abuse by clerics and efforts by bishops over many years to cover up these acts from being publicized. This information was significant enough to return to those previously interviewed and to ask them the four questions listed at the beginning of Chapter 14:

- What is your own reaction to the current situation regarding clergy abuse and the bishops' actions?
- Has it changed or affected your own attitude and/or practice regarding the Catholic Church?
- What changes are necessary in the Church, structurally or otherwise?
- What do you think Pope Francis could or should do right now in light of these recent events?

Over the course of two weeks, all fifty-two of those interviewed in 2017 were contacted and invited to respond to these four questions, either by email or through a conversation over the phone. Information was received from forty-five people (87%), sixteen from those were no longer practicing Catholics (76%), and twenty-nine who had remained in the Church (94%). The results of their input were compiled and included in "Could Be a Turning Point" in Chapter 14.

Index

Entries that correspond to individuals interviewed
in the text have been identified in boldface.

About the Author

Thomas Sweetser, SJ, originally from Minneapolis, Minnesota, is a Jesuit priest of the Upper Midwest Province. He founded the Parish Evaluation Project in 1973, where he continues to work as a facilitator and consultant to Catholic parishes across the country. His work with the Project helps pastors, staff, and lay leaders welcome people into inclusive communities, create meaningful worship experiences, foster occasions for spiritual growth, and provide opportunities for outreach and service ministries.

Fr. Sweetser is the author and co-author of many books, including *The Parish as Covenant: A Call to Pastoral Partnership* (2001), *Keeping the Covenant: Taking Parish to the Next Level* (2007), and *Changing Pastors* (1998) (with Mary Benet McKinney, OSB). After spending 31 years in Chicago, he now resides in Milwaukee at the Arrupe Jesuit Community adjacent to Marquette University.

About the Publisher

The Crossroad Publishing Company publishes Crossroad and Herder & Herder books. We offer a 200-year global family tradition of books on spiritual living and religious thought. We promote reading as a time-tested discipline for focus and understanding. We help authors shape, clarify, write, and effectively promote their ideas. We select, edit, and distribute books. With our expertise and passion, we provide wholesome spiritual nourishment for heart, mind, and soul through the written word.